MOTOR-BOATING

James Yates

Helmsman Books

First published in 1993 by
Helmsman Books, an imprint of
The Crowood Press Ltd
Ramsbury, Marlborough
Wiltshire SN8 2HR

British Library Cataloguing-in-Publication Data
A catalogue record for this book is available from the British Library.

ISBN 1 85223 761 9

Acknowledgements
The author would like to thank the following for their help and assistance in providing information and photographs for this book:

Rick Butcher of Perkins Engines Ltd, Chris Cattrall for several photographs and technical information, Jane Shimmin SRN for her invaluable contribution to the first aid section in the chapter on safety afloat, Steve Hunt of Greenacre Photographic and Bernard Martin of Lucas Rists Wiring Systems. Thanks are also due to the many manufacturers who provided illustrations of their products; their help is fully acknowledged and very much appreciated.

Line-drawings by Claire Upsdale-Jones

Throughout this book, he, his and him have been used as neutral pronouns to refer to both men and women.

Typeset by Avonset, Midsomer Norton, Bath.
Printed and bound in Great Britain by Redwood Books, Trowbridge.

CONTENTS

PREFACE

What is it about boating of any kind that engenders the spirit of adventure in the individual? The need to get afloat? The lure of a stretch of open water? Believe me, once you have been bitten by the boating bug, you will be smitten for life.

Boating is one of the fastest growing participation sports in Britain today and offers the individual or family a vast number of opportunities to suit every type, whether it is slow, lazy cruising inland or the fast cut and thrust of power-boat racing on the open sea. It is a pastime for every temperament and for all ages and sexes – everyone can participate with equal enjoyment.

To burst another great bubble myth about boating, you do not necessarily have to be a millionaire to own a boat. It will undoubtedly be expensive if you opt for a top of the range fifty-footer in hand-crafted glass-reinforced plastic (GRP)

with twin 500-horsepower turbo-charged and intercooled diesels! But if you choose a humble 20-foot second-hand cabin cruiser that has been properly looked after you could get started for a fraction of the cost and, who knows, you might even end up enjoying it more!

This book has been written to help the first-timer through the many decisions that have to be taken along the road to purchasing and actually using a boat. By the end of it you should have a better idea about the type of boating you want to do, the sort of boat you need to buy for that purpose, how to look after it and how to navigate it in safety. You will learn how to go about choosing equipment for your new boat, and how to plan a cruise and maintain the engine, but above all you will learn that boating is essentially a fun pastime and certainly one that can be enjoyed by the whole family.

1
WHY MOTORBOATING?

Boating is probably the most popular participation sport that involves the whole family and it is certain that no other sport can offer such fun and variety as do the different types of leisure boating. One minute you could find yourself gliding majestically through the pastoral countryside of the English canals with their associated locks, weirs, swing bridges and waterside pubs, while the next you could become involved in the excitement of small dinghy racing. The sting of spray and the hiss of water skis coupled with the roar of a big outboard engine might be your choice instead, or you may prefer to be cruising gently and exploring the creeks and estuaries around rugged and beautiful coastlines. For others, cruising through the Mediterranean or the network of canals in France and Holland might attract. Planning the voyage during the winter months in front of the fire, getting the stores aboard, and finally navigating, course-

For quiet, pastoral boating how about buying a narrowboat to cruise the inland waterways.

The other face of motorboating – a luxury trawler yacht-type of motorboat, capable of cruising off shore as well as undertaking some longer sea voyages.

plotting and being self-disciplined imposes a rigid self-sufficiency but brings the final reward of being at one with the elements.

Whatever form the activity you choose might take, the love of water, the sheer fun associated with the preparation of the boat, and the enthusiasm of owners, is common to all.

Skills and Resources

One of the main attractions of boating is that it can be less demanding in terms of special skills than can other sports like tennis, snooker or even football and darts! Obviously, if offshore cruising is to be taken seriously then a good background knowledge in the art and method of navigation will be required – many boating or yachting organizations will tell you all you need to know, as will books, magazines and evening classes. However, in terms of a general activity, boating makes fewer demands upon muscular fitness and strength, dedication and team spirit than do many other sports; you can just go off and do your own thing. Boating does, however, offer a realistic challenge to yourself against the elements of water and weather, and once control of these is mastered, the handling of the boat and its safe navigation will stimulate their own particular brand of pleasure and achievement.

Boating of any sort was at one time a rich man's hobby. This is no longer the case and thousands of new boaters come into the sport every year. Over the last ten years, there have been immense improvements in the ways in which you can obtain mortgages and financial help to

For many, the medium-sized GRP cruiser like this 24-foot Atlanta is the type of craft for them. It has four berths and is an ideal family boat for the first-time buyer.

buy your boat, so that many finance companies are now willing to approve loans for the purchase of new and used craft and equipment.

As I mentioned earlier, motorboating need not be an expensive hobby. True, it will cost you *some* money, but then what activity doesn't these days? It all depends upon the style of boating you opt for. It would be silly to suggest that the first-time boater should rush out and buy the first boat he comes across; there is a great deal of investigative work needed before you make your purchase. First, you must decide what you want out of your newly chosen hobby.

Start Small

I believe that it is best to start off in a small way, for you may find that you hate boating after all and have wasted time and money on something you will never use again. If your desire is simply to get afloat, then lake or canal cruising might be the answer. There are many different types of small boat from which to choose, from the humble two-berth cabin cruiser right up through a huge range of cabin, weekender and sports boats to the ultimate in fast ocean-going craft. The price you pay for these depends on many factors – the age or type of the boat, its engines and so on – but you could buy a good second-hand canal boat for the price of a cheap second-hand car or a state-of-the-art luxury power yacht capable of cruising almost anywhere on the globe for the price of a mansion.

One factor to consider when buying for the first time is how and where you are

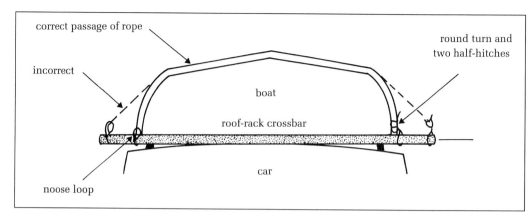

The correct method for securing a small boat on the roof-rack of a car or van. Single-bar roof-racks are the best for this job.

going to use and keep your boat. It's no use having a boat which is so heavy to carry that it will not travel safely on the roof-rack of your car (called car topping) or be manhandled from the roadside to the water's edge. Car topping is a very good way of getting the most out of small boat cruising. It opens up all sorts of cruising areas, from canals to lakes, rivers and the coast, and is a very good way for the whole family to enjoy boating. Obviously, you must be able to carry the boat

Perhaps the simplest type of boating is on board a small dinghy with an outboard; it can also be transported on the roof of a family car.

Where space is at a premium, a folding boat like this could be the answer. This model can be packed up and carried in the boot of a car or on its roof.

you choose on the roof of the car and it must be light enough to be carried by the family. There are several companies that produce packages including boat, oars, painters and outboard engine, all of which can be fitted into or on to the average family saloon.

For even greater compactness, how about a folding boat? There are several types available and all are very reasonably priced. This sort of boat can be stowed very easily and can be erected ready for use within minutes. Most are made from a combination of timbers and heavy-duty fabric cloth and are strongly built as well as being very lightweight.

For something a little more substantial, how about a lightweight marine-grade aluminium boat which has the added advantages of being relatively maintenance-free and very versatile? These boats are suitable for use on canals, rivers, lakes and coastal waters. On the best craft, all joints will be welded and not riveted, which should make for strength and durability. They will also all accept outboard motors and range from 8 feet up to 14 feet in length.

A slightly larger boat can be trailed behind the car. This one can be purchased as a package along with a 4-horsepower outboard motor and the towing trailer.

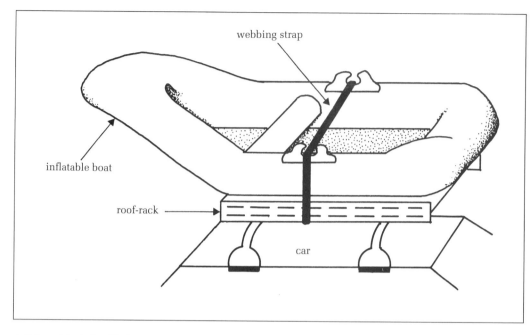

webbing strap

inflatable boat

roof-rack

car

A lightweight inflatable boat can also be carried on the roof-rack. Usually a single rope or webbing tie will be needed, but a fore and aft line will give stability.

For the raw beginner to motorboating, the outboard-powered dinghy is both a cheap and versatile introduction.

Start With a Sail

Although this book is principally about motor boats, many people start their boating careers in a sailing dinghy. Many companies make sailing dinghies for those who want to add another dimension to their boating, and craft like the Mirror and Miracle dinghies which were first introduced in the late 1960s and early 1970s have been bought by literally thousands of sailors. I started my boating with a simple marine ply home-built canoe from a Percy Blandford design. After that came a Mirror dinghy, an 18-foot cabin sloop, a 20-foot Dawncraft (another company who got many people afloat for the first time), a 36-foot steel narrow boat and a 27-foot Moody sailing

There are many sleek, fast motor boats available on the market. Many, like this Sealine, are capable of offshore cruising.

yacht. I then decided that, after all those years of being at the mercy of the wind and the tides, I would finally opt for the relative luxury of a motor boat, a boat in which I could cruise almost anywhere at anytime – weather permitting! I shall never forget the pleasure and excitement of sailing, but a good deal of that pleasure is still there when I'm cruising in my motor boat. My present boat is a 40-foot auxiliary cruiser built in timber of which I am very proud, but I still remember and will never forget the joy that I got from the launch in my local river of the *Gannet*, my first home-built boat!

For the best of both worlds, a small motor-sailer like this Hardy can be trailed, sailed or motored using a small auxiliary outboard engine.

An inflatable boat is another safe and reasonably economical method of getting afloat. Your cruising grounds will be limited mainly to canals, rivers or estuaries, but the boats can usually be carried simply in the boot of a small car.

SUMMARY

- Boating is probably the most popular participation sport which involves the whole family and it is certain that no other sport can offer such fun and variety as do the different types of leisure boating.

- One of the main attractions of boating is that it can be less demanding in terms of special skills than can other sports like tennis, snooker or even football and darts!

- Boating of any sort was at one time a rich man's hobby. This is no longer the case and thousands of new boaters come into the sport every year.

- There are many different types of small boat from which to choose, from the humble two-berth cabin cruiser right up through a huge range of cabin, weekender and sports boats to the ultimate in fast ocean-going craft.

2
A BOAT FOR ALL REASONS

Let us assume that you have decided which sort of boating is for you and (probably more important still) that you have or can arrange the means to pay for the activity. The next step is actually to choose the boat. As I have already said, there are many boats on the market all vying with each other for a place in the boat showroom. So, how do you actually go about choosing? Well, there are several ways. One is to visit the big boat shows which take place at various venues on an annual basis. The three biggest shows in the UK are the London International which is centred on the Earls Court Exhibition Hall in central London in early January, the Southampton Boat Show which runs for ten days in the third week of September and the East Coast Boat Show which is held over five days in Ipswich in May or June. Personally, I prefer the Southampton show as many of the new boats exhibited are actually afloat and available for evaluation in their natural element. This gives a much better idea of exactly what the boat can do and how it looks on the water – something difficult to visualise in the confines of even a giant-sized exhibition hall. The London show, I feel, is much better for choosing smaller craft like dinghies, tenders and inflatables, as well as the myriad

boating accessories that go to make a boat fit for cruising.

The boating press is another place to do some serious looking. All the popular boating magazines advertise a good selection of new boats, all backed up with in-depth tests and reports. They also have substantial brokerage and second-hand classified sections at the back. Some really good bargains can be had from these pages, and I urge you to study them carefully.

One thing to bear in mind when looking through magazines is price. Many cruisers built for seagoing use have wider beams and draughts than boats designed for the river or inland waterway system and this, coupled with the larger engines involved, can really bump up the sale price. If you wish to restrict your boating to canals, rivers or lakes then much cheaper boating is available, with the boats having just as much comfort and style as those built for use on the sea.

Second-Hand Boats

The way many boat owners begin their boating lives is by buying a second-hand cruiser and perhaps one that needs a bit of work. If this is your intention, steer away

One of the pleasures of boat ownership is carrying out the care and maintenance that is necessary in order to keep the boat and its equipment in tip-top, safe condition.

from the glossy marina showrooms and seek out some of the back-creek boat-yards, the classified advertisements of your local evening paper or journals dedicated to the sale of used boats; all of these have some excellent second-hand bargains available. If you are adept at DIY then so much the better, for the practical maintenance of a boat is part and parcel of the enjoyment of ownership and you will find many bargains to be had which require improvement work. By applying some rudimentary carpentry, electrical and mechanical skills a good deal of money can be saved. Buying a used boat also gives you the opportunity to redesign it so that you can tailor the interior to suit your personal requirements.

Surveyors

One of the golden rules when considering buying any type of second-hand boat is to have a proper survey carried out by a qualified marine surveyor (this is covered in greater detail in Chapter 5, *see* page 69). It might add to the final bill, but is well worth it in terms of peace of mind and the knowledge that you have not spent your hard-earned cash on a sieve!

There are several good and reputable marine surveyors about and most are prepared to travel long distances to view and assess a boat on your behalf. Believe me, when it comes to choosing between getting a sound boat with value for money or being saddled with a leaking, osmosis-

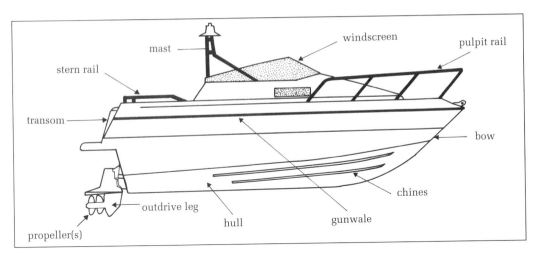

The main parts of a motor boat.

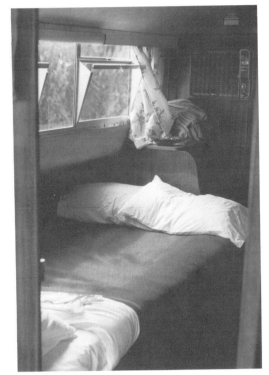

Many modern boats are fitted out to high standards with comfortable, welcoming interiors.

ridden heap of junk with a clapped-out engine. I know which road I would take.

Another good reason for having a survey carried out is that many finance and insurance companies – some of whom have really had their fingers burnt in the last few years – are now reluctant to part with any money or insure a boat without sight of a bona fide surveyor's report.

Comfortable Interiors

Whichever type of boat you eventually choose you will, in almost every case, end up with some form of comfortable interior. Gone are the days when the small cruising boat provided only very basic needs for a rather cramped and spartan existence afloat. Glass-fibre mouldings now provide many of the built-in comforts of home, with lockers, a full galley, toilets and even showers. Advances in insulation materials have also meant that boats these days are warm and

15

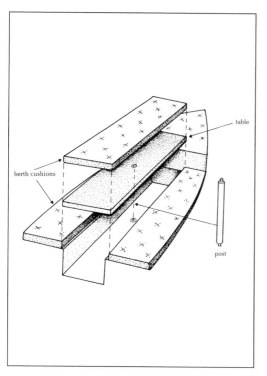

One of the most popular methods of converting single berths into a roomier double in smaller boats is to lower the central table and fit an infill cushion in the gap.

Take Care!

It is wise to take care when choosing your boat as the initial attraction and the sudden impulse to buy can seduce the unwary into making a rash purchase that may sour their feelings towards boating forever. While it is very easy to make a purchase, especially from an unscrupulous boat salesman who is desperate to make a sale of any sort, careful thought and assessment are needed before you decide upon the most suitable type of boat for your needs.

A good salesman who handles a range of several types and sizes of craft will, by process of elimination and evaluation, be able to assess the right type of boat for you, but it is always far better if you can decide these factors for yourself before you even enter the showroom. That way you can look into the market more deeply and at specific types of cruiser rather than at the complete market of small, large, luxury, river, canal or offshore boats.

For a raw newcomer to boating it will be wise to read all the literature cautiously and apply a little common sense. Start by asking yourself a series of questions – something any good salesman should do if you go to him for advice.

Relative Costs

It is interesting when talking to people in the boating trade and to people who do not own a boat just what their perception is of the cost of a boat. Some people want a luxury craft with all the extras for the price of a canoe, while others have the impression that a small trailable boat costs as much as a house! I know that these are slight exaggerations, but they do

condensation-free. There are also pressurised hot water systems, flush toilets and even central heating, with the options of colour television, video and microwave ovens so that boats can be better equipped than some houses!

For many, this sort of luxury is just a pipe-dream and the majority of boat owners are content with the basics of a sound, seaworthy craft with good cooking, washing and sleeping facilities. These boat owners still enjoy their hobby to the full and at the same time retain some control on costs.

There is no need to slum it when afloat – most motor boats are now fitted with full galleys. This galley is aboard a larger river cruiser, but facilities on smaller craft are still more than adequate for the preparation of meals.

Extending the cruising range of a boat can be achieved by buying a trailable model. You are limited to size, but holidays afloat can be varied – you can even take the boat abroad.

illustrate the extremes of thinking. The important thing is to determine accurately a figure that you can afford – both in terms of initial purchase and of subsequent running costs – and then stick to it.

There are many permutations of both boat and price, and once again there is no substitute for doing a bit of research in the boating magazines and by visiting boat-yards and manufacturers. To illustrate the variations, I cover below the main types of craft, detailing general size, accommodation and facilities and the areas in which you will be most likely to cruise. The categories covered are: trailable boats, canal and river boats (cruisers only; narrowboats are different altogether), off-shore cruisers, fishing boats, and sports boats.

Trailable Boats

Trailable boats are one of the largest sectors of the cruiser market, due mainly to their cost and flexibility of use. You will find boats within this category in all types of waters mainly because of their size – normally 20 feet or less with a beam that will still negotiate narrow canal systems if required (usually 6 feet 8 inches).

Trailable boats will usually accommodate two adults in the forward cabin, the larger types also having a facility to sleep a further two in the cockpit under a canvas or PVC canopy. The standard fittings of these smaller craft are fairly basic with two berths and, depending on the design, a two-burner cooker, a hand basin and small portable chemical toilet. Once you get into the larger end of the range, however, the facilities offered aboard tend to improve, with such items as a separate toilet compartment with a door or curtain

to screen it from the rest of the cabin, and the installation of a full two-burner cooker with grill and oven, plus storage compartments and drawers.

The limitations to trailable craft are usually confined to weight and ease of launching and recovery. The weight is limited to what your towing vehicle can safely pull, but this is usually within the $\frac{3}{4}$–$1\frac{1}{4}$-ton range. The average 1,600cc family car will comfortably tow a ton in weight, while the bigger and more powerful vehicles such as four-wheel drives and estate cars will obviously tow heavier craft. You must, however, remember that when towing a boat you are subject to different road traffic rules; make sure you are familiar with them.

Despite the above limitations a trailable boat can be very flexible and great fun once it is on the water. Most are suitable for fishing, pottering about, water-skiing or as a waterborne version of a sports car. It is in this area that their flexibility comes to the fore, as most are fitted with outboard engines and you buy the engine, or engines, to suit the use you require for the boat. On rivers or for fishing off the coast an economical 15–25 horsepower motor is sufficient, but if you intend to water-ski then a power unit of 70 horsepower upwards may be needed. If you intend boating off the coast it is always advisable to have a second power unit for emergencies; this need only be a small outboard unit that has sufficient power to give the boat headway should the main engine break down.

There are many boat showrooms and boat-yards that stock this size of cruiser, and both boat builders' and manufacturers' advertisements, and the classified advertisement pages in boating magazines, will reveal many outlets. The sales

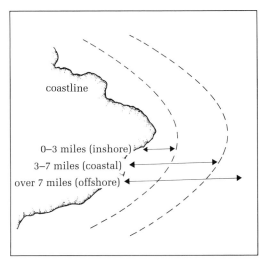

coastline

0–3 miles (inshore)
3–7 miles (coastal)
over 7 miles (offshore)

The differences between inshore, coastal and offshore cruising.

staff at these dealers' showrooms will be able to advise you on the various aspects of each type and size of craft, suitable outboard engines, trailers, and equipment to have on board. It is well worth going to see several of those in your area as they may offer a number of bargains either in boats or engines – or indeed a drive-away package of a boat with both engine and trailer.

Another good reason for opting for a trailable boat – especially if budget is a key factor – is one of storage. Within reason, you can keep the boat on its trailer in your driveway at home or in a lock-up garage near by. By doing this, the boat will always be conveniently placed for maintenance work and you will not have to pay out expensive mooring fees for those

The outboard motor is a versatile method of propulsion for the smaller boat.

The wide-beam glass-fibre cruiser is ideal for cruising rivers or wetland areas. They might look ungainly, but they are exceptionally spacious and very comfortable.

At the top end of the market a luxury offshore motor boat like this Fairline 35, powered by twin inboard diesel engines, will take you almost anywhere.

months that the boat is not in use. However, first check any local planning regulations or by-laws which might restrict you from parking a boat in front of your property.

Canal and River Boats

Boats for canal and river use are divided roughly into two types: those that have been built specially for the river and those that are equally at home on river or sea. Boats in the first category differ slightly from the coastal versions in that they have shallower draughts so that they can cruise most parts of canal systems or rivers – even the upper reaches where shallower water is often found. They are also usually much roomier inside, with a wide beam and spacious saloon that have been designed for relaxing cruising without having to pay due regard to the possible rough weather situations that may be experienced at sea.

Some of these cruisers can appear a little snub-nosed and ungainly in appearance, but what they lack in styling is more than made up for in interior spaciousness. One very good way of trying out such craft is to hire one for a short holiday. Many such production boats that can be hired on inland waterways can also be bought as new or used craft. If the river is for you, then one of these might be your ideal boat. Holiday boat hire brochures are packed full of boats of all sizes and styles for hire on lake systems as well as canals.

Several cruisers are equally at home on the sea and on the quieter waters of the rivers. Boats such as those in the Sealine range can accommodate up to four adults in comfortable, designer surroundings and have a wide variety of power units available from single diesel engines through to twin installations of either petrol or diesel. You should remember that although many first-timers start their boating careers on the rivers, a high percentage progress through estuary cruising to full coastal and offshore cruising when they become proficient. The choice of craft at the initial stage may well dictate the feasibility of such cruising at a later date when more powerful engines may be required. Just because a new boat is fitted with one type of engine does not mean that it cannot have a replacement unit later on – providing that the class of boat and hull design will stand it.

There are many good production boats available for river cruising which offer a wide variety of accommodation, styles and facilities. Many boat builders have ranges of glass-fibre craft capable of cruising rivers, and the smaller ones will be suitable for canals as well. The engine combinations are also wide and encompass both outboard and inboard options. Each manufacturer has a chain of dealerships and sales outlets which will provide back-up service and assistance with the running of your boat.

Offshore Cruisers

When choosing a boat for use off shore or for coastal cruising you will find the range just as wide. Many of the manufacturers of canal and river boats also sell boats capable of withstanding the extra rigours that a sea voyage will put upon their hulls, superstructure and equipment. Once again, glass-reinforced plastic (GRP) or glass fibre is by far and away the most popular material for seagoing craft, although there are also many boats constructed from timber, steel and ferro-cement. These materials are described fully in Chapter 3 (*see* page 32).

Most standard production boat builders catering for the coastal market build a range of craft from around 25 feet up to 50 feet, usually in 25-, 32-, 37-, 42-, 47- and 50-feet sizes. Most have twin diesel or petrol engine installations and either a standard propeller shaft driving a propeller or an outdrive unit where the power take-off from the engine's gearbox is transferred through special gearing to a leg that is attached to the transom of the boat.

Again, it is very much a personal choice as to the standards of comfort, quality of fittings and interior design, but as far as sea-keeping abilities go, there are few differences between comparable boats. There is no substitute for a good nose around at a boat show, preferably a water-based one where you may be able to try out and evaluate the boats in your chosen category on the water.

If you intend to cruise as a family, try to involve the other members in the decision-making process as much as possible. Make every member feel that he is contributing a point of view – even the children. In this way you will have your family on your side from the word go as they will feel that they are involved in the hobby. They will feel that they will have had their say about comfort, cabin space, sleeping arrangements and stowage, as well as the lay-out of the galley and the essential toilet! If your spouse and children feel that they have helped you choose the boat, they will be much more likely to want to cruise with you on a regular basis.

Not all modern cruisers are standard production craft. There are many good individual boat builders who will make you a one-off design exactly to your specifications. However, you must expect to pay a premium for such a boat, and although you will have a craft of individuality it might be wise to wait a few years and build up some experience of being afloat and living aboard before finally committing so much money to your ultimate dream.

Fishing Boats

If you are interested in sea fishing as a hobby then you might well appreciate some of the available boats that lend themselves readily to rod and line. These cruisers are usually capable of sleeping at least two adults aboard in reasonable comfort, whilst others offer a great deal in the way of luxurious comfort.

Quite a few of the small trailable boats fit into this category and have reasonably sized aft cockpits – which are absolutely essential if serious sea fishing is contemplated. More traditional working-style fishing boats and fast fisher/cruisers are also available, so, again, it is worth investigating all the options before making your final choice.

Sports Boats

These are the boats at the fast end of the leisure market, the sort that are often seen in James Bond films where sleek, low speedboats are used to chase the villain! Appealing mainly to the younger boat enthusiast, these craft nevertheless offer a combination of boating styles. For a start, most sports boats can easily be trailed behind the family car, they can be used not only for high-speed cruising but also to pull a water-skier, and some even have small cabins which provide their owners

If fishing is your forte, why not take your favourite sport afloat? This Alaska boat from Shetland has a wide, open stern ideal for five or six fishermen plus their tackle.

Younger boat owners may prefer a fast, open sports boat. These craft can be fun as they run at speed as well as allowing such activities as water-skiing and parascending.

with comfortable, if rudimentary, accommodation – suitable for a couple of nights over a weekend.

Most sports cruisers are sleek in appearance and design, with greater emphasis placed on performance and speed than accommodation. Big, powerful engines dominate the centre and aft sections, as do their large fuel tanks, and because of this the overall cost of sports boating can be much higher than low-speed cruising.

There are many sports boats on the market, many of them manufactured in America or Australia. Careful choice can get you a bargain, and you may be able to negotiate an engine, boat and trailer package deal.

Plan Your Search

Before buying any sort of boat, I would suggest that you buy a few copies of some of the many monthly boating magazines, which will give you some insight into the various types of cruising or sports boats available and boating activity in general. By doing this you will become familiar with what is on the market and what can be achieved within the limitations of your budget and perceived skill. Start by looking at the many advertisements for boats, and then send off for manufacturers' brochures and price lists so that you can get a realistic idea of what each type of boat is likely to cost. A good source of brochure information is one of the boat shows, but be prepared to take a large carrier bag!

In many ways, looking for a boat is no different from researching next year's holiday brochures – except that by buying a boat you could also be buying your holidays over the next few years! This is actually something you might like to bear in mind when contemplating buying a boat – work out how much you spend on family holidays each year, multiply it by, say, ten (years) and then add on a bit for inflation. Against that figure of what you would normally expect to pay for a couple of weeks' holiday each year, consider that if you spend it on a boat you could look forward to not only two weeks, but several weeks and quite a few weekends afloat for years to come.

New or Used

Having first decided on the type and size of boat to suit your requirements, the next major consideration is whether to buy new or used. This decision should be tempered by the construction material of any cruiser under review.

The vast majority of cruisers built today – even the large, 45- to 50-footers – are constructed from GRP mouldings, although there are still a few that are constructed of timber, steel or, occasionally, aluminium. GRP has played a great part in tempering the prices of standard production motor cruisers – without it many of us would not be able to afford to buy a boat at all. It is strong and flexible and, if damaged, relatively easy to repair. I talk about GRP at length in Chapter 3 (*see* page 38) but basically the material has a degree of flexibility that will absorb some pressure on impact without cracking or breaking up and will contain that impact pressure in a local area; timber planking or steel plate can spring on impact so that a larger area of the vessel is affected.

Buying New

The advantages of buying new are no different from those you would experience when buying a new car or house. The main advantage is that you have a manufacturer's warranty, both on the vessel itself and also on the individual pieces of equipment installed aboard. Engines, radios, radar, navigational equipment and installations right through to the toilet units will each have their own manufacturer's warranty, although as most of these are transferred to the boat builder it is up to him to arrange for any malfunction to be corrected.

You also start off with a brand new cruiser with interior décor and colourings chosen by you, albeit from a set of patterns and colours if it is a production boat. You can also choose any additional extras that you want to have fitted right down to the size of the engines. If you are having a boat custom built then the latter advantages are even more marked than on a production vessel. You can also have a standard production hull and superstructure individually fitted out – the choice is yours!

All of the major production boat builders in the UK are members of the SBBNF (Ship and Boat Builders' National Federation) who have a code of practice for the construction of craft; many also construct to comply with the stringent Lloyds A1 Certificate. If you are buying a cruiser for river use make sure that it has been constructed to comply with any other special regulations that local authorities and waterway boards insist upon. These regulations deal mainly with safety aspects of boats in terms of the engine, fuel and gas installations as well as with fire-fighting equipment. They are there for a purpose and should not be ignored. In fact, if your boat is lacking in these standards upon inspection, a licence to cruise the waterway may be refused. In any case, it is as well to ask – especially if you are buying a new boat.

The final advantage of buying new is that it is easier to obtain funding either from a bank or a finance company that deals in either marine mortgages or marine finance, subject to your own personal circumstances.

Buying Second-Hand

Buying a used craft entails considerably more experience in knowing just what to look for and in assessing if a good buy is all that it appears to be. This subject is looked at in detail in Chapter 5 (*see* page 69).

If you are entering the marine field for the first time it might be safer to make your first used boat purchase from a reputable marine dealer – someone you can go back to should things start to go wrong with the boat shortly after you have purchased it. You should also study the classified columns of the boating press, including the brokerage pages, for the type of cruiser that you have decided is suitable to your requirements. That way you can put together a picture of what each type of boat is likely to fetch, depending on how old it is. Again, the similarity to the used-car market is apparent in that you will be able to ascertain that used craft handled by dealers are priced a little higher than those offered for sale privately. With both cars and boats this is invariably because the dealer has to be able to offer a back-up sales service.

What should you look for in a used

cruiser and what must you not be misled by? On some craft you will find a mahogany or oak board fastened to a main bulkhead with a series of numbers deeply engraved into it. That will show that the boat has been entered as a British Registered Vessel, in exactly the same manner as a house or property is entered on the Land Register. It will only tell you who currently owns the craft and give you details about it as they appeared at the time of registration; it is not a commitment as to the state and condition of the craft as it is now.

If you are buying from a reputable dealer it is in his own interests to ensure that you are made fully aware of the exact condition of any used cruiser you buy from him. Those dealers that are well established and are still operating have only managed to do so on the strength of their trading practice and reputation. But that still does not alter your right to bring in an independent marine surveyor to give the vessel the once-over if you so wish. When you are spending a lot of money on a used craft it is only prudent to seek expert advice as to that craft's condition and seaworthiness. The money spent on a survey could save you much more at a later date, and you need only commit yourself to having a survey done when you think that you have found the craft to suit your needs and pocket.

A point well worth remembering here is that a gleaming cruiser is the sign of a careful competent owner to the untrained eye. But is it in fact just a cosmetic job to cover up a multitude of existing problems or potential problems later on? It is at these times that you really need a surveyor who is accustomed to looking beyond the exterior to the state and condition of the boat as a whole.

Once you decide to buy a used boat rather than a new one you must also be prepared to travel around the country in order to get just what you are looking for. Unlike motor cars, cruisers are relatively few in number, and their mooring or storage points are also much further apart than the local garages. Some areas are different in that there are more marinas or boating facilities linked together in a small area, but a small amount spent on motoring around may save you a lot and may get you a far better buy

The Decision!

We now come to the crunch point – decision time. Is the boat really what you want? Does it offer enough room for all the crew? Is the whole family happy with the choice of boat? Finally, was that day or half-day really enough time in which adequately to assess the boat? You will probably still have little doubts as to whether or not you are making the correct decision, but the answer is relatively simple – hire it first!

Try Hiring

The cost of a week's or a few days' hire of a boat compared to the sum lost over the first few months if you find yourself having to sell off an unwanted cruiser will be very different! If the boat-yard you have been negotiating with for the purchase of a boat does not have a hire fleet or will not let you hire out either the cruiser you are thinking of buying or a similar one then start looking around for one that will oblige you.

With most types of standard production motor cruisers you will find a hire/charter

Before you part with your money, find out if a life afloat is really for you by hiring a boat for a week or two, perhaps on safe, easy waters.

fleet based on a major river. Some boat-yards also welcome the opportunity to show you over their cruisers and firmly believe that it is only over a period of time that you are fully able to assess a cruiser. More importantly for you (the potential buyer) is that should you take up the offer of a week's hire – a holiday in itself – and should you subsequently purchase a similar cruiser from that boat-yard, then the yard may well refund the hire cost against the cost of the new boat. This way, at worst you will have spent some money in order to try out a cruiser for size and fit and have had a week's holiday afloat, but at best if you decide to buy then the week's holiday will have cost you no-thing. This accommodating attitude of

some boat-yards is on the increase, es-pecially when they are marketing production or semi-production luxury cruisers that have steadily built up their reputations over the years.

A final good point which comes from this experience is very important for a new owner. Hire fleet boats gain more use in one season than a private boat will in nearly ten seasons. Their cruisers are on the move continuously for eight months of the year, being handled by dozens and dozens of different helmsmen – some good, others not so good – in all weathers. You will therefore gain some experience of how the boat will age. The service records of a good hire fleet will also readily show just how reliable their

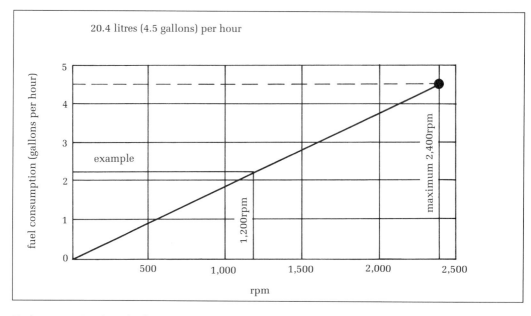

Fuel consumption for a displacement boat. At displacement speeds, fuel used at 1,200rpm is around 10.4 litres (2.3 gallons) per hour and at the average maximum cruising speed of 2,400rpm it rises to 20.4 litres (4.5 gallons) per hour.

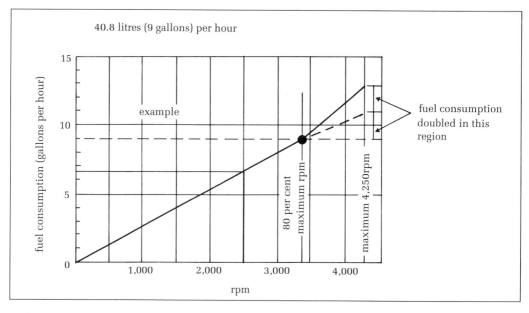

Fuel consumption on a high-speed planing craft. Note that the fuel consumption rises rapidly at higher engine speeds.

Moorings

Finding a location in which to moor your boat after you have bought it is becoming more and more difficult each year. Many coast-based marinas have long waiting lists for the few spare berths that are available, but investment in new marinas and extending existing ones is progressing. Canal networks are a little better in terms of the number of moorings available, and there are also usually secure moorings to be had at boat-yards as well as certain numbers of private moorings. Before making your final selection, consideration must be given to a number of points; choose your site carefully and check the facilities offered.

On some lakes you will find that many of the moorings are privately owned or belong to the local boat-yards. These moorings rarely come up for use by 'outsiders' and are guarded jealously. If you have purchased your boat through a boat-yard or marina the company will usually do its best to provide you with a mooring to go with your craft. Indeed, some craft are sold along with an option to moor on site – a very useful bonus. Most moorings are situated up rivers or creeks in the case of coastal sites, or alongside rivers, canals or lakes, and usually in basins off the main waterway or on staging in the main stream.

In quiet areas you are likely to find simple staging comprising planks attached to sunken scaffolding or piles to which you can moor the boat. Many marinas, especially those located in tidal waters, are equipped with floating pontoon moorings. These are buoyant steel tanks topped with hardwood timber planking incorporating galvanized cleats for tying up the boat and are much more

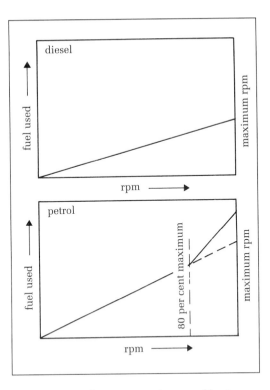

The comparison between petrol-powered boats and those using diesel fuel. It can be seen that diesel-powered craft use fuel in a relatively linear way for any given engine rpm, but on a petrol-fuelled boat the consumption rises dramatically at about 80 per cent power.

cruisers are in operation and a proud owner will willingly show off his service records to you. If he is not too happy about letting you see them then start looking hard at another yard or a different make of boat.

A glance at the latest brochures from boat holiday booking agencies and individual hire firms will show you which fleets operate which craft to help you search for a suitable boat-yard from which to hire.

CHOICE OF MOORING

- Do you want to cruise coastal areas, rivers or canals?

- Does the area around the marina appeal to your family?

- Is the marina or boat-yard far from home? If it is, are you prepared for the long drive each time you want to go to the boat?

- Does the boat-yard have a good security system – twenty-four hour watchmen, locked gates and some form of customer/boat identification system?

- If the marina is in a remote area will it affect your insurance premium?

- Is there a good range of facilities close to hand?

- Is there a secure car-park?

Now you have bought your boat, where are you going to keep it? There are several options, the most popular being the pontoon marina.

secure. In tidal marinas they also rise and fall with the tide, keeping the boats moored to them safe and level. Moorings such as this give access to cruising at all states of the tide, which is an important consideration when you look at the overall costs of using and maintaining a boat.

Tidal Moorings

Moorings in the estuary of a river also have to take into account the rise and fall of the tide. Some moorings will usually be available at the shore side, but these tend to dry out and are really suitable only for boats fitted with bilge keels where the hull will remain on a level plane at low water. Many new marinas and those that utilize old sea basins or docks are controlled by a special lock that allows the boat to remain afloat at all times. The lock will allow access to the sea only at certain times either side of high water.

Another choice of mooring is the trot or swinging mooring. These are special mooring chains that are anchored by a concrete block to the sea-bed. Once again, these tend to dry out at low water and so are suitable only for bilge keelers, although you may be able to find some deep-water swinging moorings that keep the boat afloat at all states of the tide, night or day. The disadvantage of this type of mooring is that access to and from the boat necessitates a trip in a dinghy or tender which is either left tied to the mooring or hoisted aboard the main vessel.

SUMMARY

- One way of choosing a boat is to visit the big boat shows which take place at various venues on an annual basis.

- Many cruisers built for seagoing use have wider beams and draughts than boats designed for the river or inland waterways system, and this, coupled with the larger engines involved, can really bump up the sale price.

- Glass-fibre mouldings now provide many of the built-in comforts of home, with lockers, a full galley, toilets and even showers.

- Will you be paying with ready cash or with the aid of finance facilities? It is always prudent to bear in mind what you can really afford and not to stretch your budget to the absolute limit.

- A good reason for opting for a trailable boat – especially if budget is a key factor – is one of storage. Within reason, you can keep the boat on its trailer in your driveway at home or in a lock-up garage near by.

3
CONSTRUCTION MATERIALS

Let us now look at some of the different materials used in boat building, the construction of the main types of motor boat and how the different hull shapes perform in the water. You should then have a much better understanding and feel of the type of boat you will need to look at before buying.

The different materials used in the construction of boats have been the subject of continuous development across the centuries, from the simple hollowed-out tree to the sophisticated glass-fibre craft of today. There are now basically five types of material still used in boat building: wood, steel, aluminium, ferro-cement and fibreglass. The choice of material is usually dictated by costs. In days gone by when labour and materials were plentiful and cheap, timber was used extensively as a boat-building medium; today it is still possible to have a timber-built motor boat custom made to your requirements, but only at great cost. Although several com-

There are still many boats around which are made entirely from timber. However, as this example shows, the maintenance of a timber boat can have an extensive draining effect upon the finances of its owner. Constant maintenance is required in almost all cases, with remedial repairs being expensive.

A close-up of some rot damage on the side of the hull of a timber cruiser. Until prodded with a screwdriver, this hull looked fine, but you never know what lurks behind the paintwork.

panies produce smaller sailing craft and dinghies in a variety of timbers, the revolution brought about by the use of fibreglass has meant that almost all production boats available in Britain, Europe and the USA are invariably constructed of glass fibre or glass-reinforced plastic (commonly abbreviated to GRP).

Timber

Boats constructed of wood, and there are still plenty around in the second-hand market as well as those lovingly cared for by owners far and wide, are usually based on several well-known boat-building methods. Some of these methods – such as carvel and clinker – are very old. Carvel design is where long planks of wood are fitted together with their edges flush over an internal framework of other

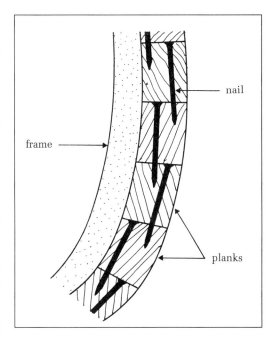

Some timber hulls use close-fitting planks which are edge-nailed to each other.

33

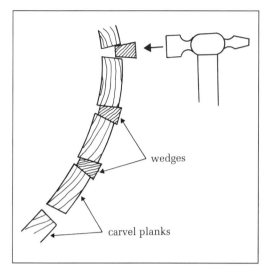

A method of sealing a carvel-planked hull by knocking in wooden wedges between the planks.

timbers based around a sturdy central backbone or keel. The framework is normally made up of hardwood and can be sawn to shape or bent using special steam chests, some of which are still in use today. The outside planks which form the hull skin can also be steam-bent to shape or physically bent to the frames where they are attached with nails to the framework below. Because the wooden planks tend to shrink and swell in water and with changes in temperature, the seams between the planks have to be sealed or plugged with a flexible, waterproof material. Traditionally this has been cotton or special putty known as caulking, and it is hammered into the joints using a special caulking iron. The finished carvel hull form is strong but it does require a good deal of maintenance and is now a very rare method of modern motor-boat construction.

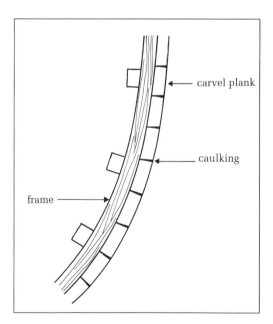

An older method of sealing a carvel-planked hull is to use caulking, a cotton-like material that is soaked in a tarry substance and forced into the seams between the planks.

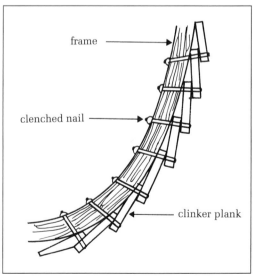

A clinker-planked hull. The planks are overlapped and are held to the frames by clenched nails.

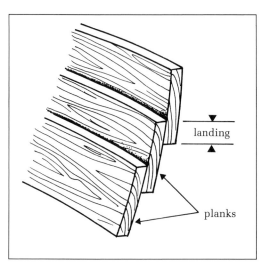

The overlap on a clinker-planked hull is called the landing.

Clinker hulls are usually made on a lighter framework with the planking overlapped slightly one on the other, a little bit like a larch-lap fence. They are fixed to the frames using rivets, screws or special copper boat nails, and are usually sealed with a special compound. The strength to weight ratio is quite good and general maintenance is lower than carvel hulls because the need for caulking is eliminated. Older craft built this way can, however, leak very badly as the wood shrinks and becomes old. The clinker hull looks very good afloat with its fine, traditional lines and is sometimes reproduced on modern cruisers by being moulded in fibreglass. The overlapped planking also creates a built-in stability as well as tending to turn spray down and away from the hull.

Plywood

In recent times, plywood has been used in timber boat building mainly in two forms: moulded and sheets. In a moulded plywood hull, layers of laminated plywood which have been shaped using heat and special resin glues are fitted over the framework of the hull. Plywood used in this way can give an excellent, strong hull that is both lightweight and simple to maintain. The look of such a boat is very similar to that of a fibreglass boat, although the plywood does have slightly less strength than GRP in the event of a direct impact.

Sheet plywood boats usually come in kit form for finishing at home. Confined mainly to smaller craft such as sailing dinghies and small power boats, this is an ideal way for the DIY boat owner to get himself afloat on a budget. The sheets are usually precut to shape and the complete kit of parts includes frames, keel, hull and superstructure. It is put together using copper clinch nails, brass screws and wood glue. The canoe that I mentioned at the beginning of this book (*see* page 10) was constructed from a kit and was a sturdy, if somewhat heavy, boat which required little maintenance and which lasted me for many years.

Steel

The general apathy towards steel boat building is now much less than it used to be. However, there are still far more GRP boats sold than steel ones even though a boat constructed of the latter, if put together properly, can have one of the strongest hulls available. I have seen many steel hulls that have suffered impact damage that would have resulted in a glass-fibre or wooden boat being sunk or damaged beyond repair. The main

Probably the most durable of all boat-building materials, steel is initially expensive but can outlast GRP and is highly suitable in situations where the boat may be knocked about – for example, in commercial craft.

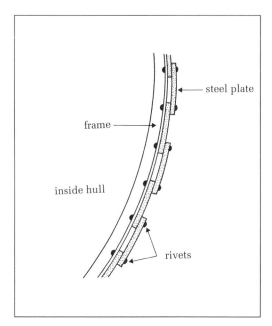

A joggled frame made up of steel plates riveted to the metal frames of the hull.

reason steel boats are not popular is that there was a scare about corrosion. Rusting on some early boats caused many manufacturers to rethink their strategies and resulted in lost orders and a general loss of confidence in the boat-buying public. But with modern techniques such as shot blasting, priming and epoxy painting these problems have almost been eradicated, with excellent hulls available in both finished and kit form which look as good as, if not better in the water than some GRP hulls. The Dutch manufacturers in particular have got this quality control, reliability and hull shaping down to a fine art. A steel hull is proportionally more expensive than a similar sized boat built from GRP, but the inherent strength and general seaworthiness make the extra expense well worth while, especially for the serious ocean-going boat owner.

It has been said that the only boat which could be built successfully from steel would have an angular shape with a chined construction, but modern bending and rolling machinery and quality welding techniques have a great bearing on the lines and finish of steel boats, their performance and their resistance to the ravages of weather and salt water.

Aluminium

Aluminium is not used as a mass boat-building material owing mainly to the expense involved in large boat construction. It is, however, used in small, mass-produced boats such as open punts, dinghies and skiffs. Because of the obvious weight savings it also makes for an ideal small boat for carrying on the car roof-rack. In the USA, aluminium is used extensively for the open fishing boat market where light weight and strength are combined to give a competitively priced general-purpose boat. Aluminium has an enormous strength to weight ratio and is almost corrosion-free, the only exception being when it is in contact with unlike metals in the salt water environment – then galvanic or electrolytic corrosion results. It can easily be moulded and formed, and is usually designed around a folded seam principle with flush rivets used to keep the hull together.

The maintenance of such a craft is also minimal and it does not even require painting, apart from an occasional lick of antifouling. The biggest drawback is that there are few boats of a reasonable size (unless you go right up market), due to the aforementioned costliness of the material.

The aluminium boat is both strong and lightweight. It is normally held together with a combination of rivets and some welded seams.

Ferro-cement

Ferro-cement was introduced in the mid-1960s and is still looked on as a rather off-beat method of boat construction. Basically, it is a fairly inexpensive construction material when used in craft over 30 feet in length where weight is not a major consideration. A complex framework is first constructed of metal tubing and mesh similar to that used in reinforced concrete in buildings. A special concrete mix is then trowelled on to the mesh and is allowed to cure and harden. Applied by a master, the resultant hull shape is comparable to that of a GRP boat. Usually seen on large ocean-going racing yachts, the main advantage is the relatively cheap construction costs.

Glass-Fibre

The type of boat most commonly seen afloat around coastlines and on inland waterways is made from glass fibre, sometimes called glass-reinforced plastic (GRP).

The first production glass-fibre boats were made in the mid-1960s and were credited with the added bonus that they would be maintenance-free. Since then, although glass-fibre technology has improved considerably, no one now believes that a boat made of glass-reinforced plastic will be totally immune to any problems. Regular maintenance work has to be undertaken every year, even if it just means giving the hull a polish or touching up chipped laminate. The basic construction of a glass-fibre boat comprises several individual parts that range from fragile to some very robust assemblies in which we entrust our lives, so it is no

By far the most popular material used for boats available from the production line is glass fibre or GRP. It is a durable, hard-wearing substance that, if well looked after, remains in an excellent condition.

great hardship to do some basic maintenance work.

No one really knows how long a fibreglass boat will last, and it is conceivable that the hull and superstructure may well outlive the majority of the fixtures and fittings installed in and on it! But perhaps due to some incorrect practices in the original construction of the boat, environmental influences, and the basic wear and tear each is subjected to, every glass-fibre craft will have a different lifespan and, as a result, will require various degrees of maintenance.

The Material

Polyester resin, which although hard when cured, has little inherent strength. It is the rather soft and pliable synthetic fibres that provide the overall strength in a moulding. When fused together the fibres and resin have a high strength to weight ratio with a splendid resistance to water absorption. The finished product – referred to as 'glass' – needs to be moulded into the boat shape. So, how does a builder mould a GRP boat into shape? To do this he must first devote a great deal of time and effort to making a plug or pattern of the required boat – this pattern is usually made out of wood. From this plug a mould like a large jelly mould (which is really a glass-fibre boat) is made. Only then can the builder start to make a complete boat.

Construction

First the inside of the mould is painted with a non-stick release agent, just as you would grease a large baking tin. This is followed by a coat of either clear or coloured special resin which will become the gelcoat outer layer or 'skin' of the new boat. After sheets of glass-fibre matting have been spread inside the mould they are either sprayed or brushed with resin, and then rolled using a special metal roller until all the glass is thoroughly soaked. After this first coat of resin-impregnated fibreglass has set, additional layers of fibreglass are positioned inside the mould and treated with resin. The process is repeated until the desired hull thickness has been reached. The new boat is then left for a time to cure, before being removed from the mould for trimming and fitting out. Because a cruiser has a cabin, its manufacture usually requires at least two moulds, one for the hull and one for the superstructure.

The gelcoat outer skin of the glass-fibre

A hull mould being laid up with a spraying machine. The machine sprays a mixture of chopped strands of glass fibre which have been impregnated with special resin.

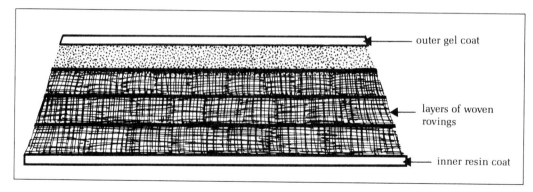

The layered construction of a glass-fibre boat.

boat looks smooth and shiny, but it is much more than a cosmetic finish. It is usually about 0.05 of an inch thick and must be completely free from any air bubbles. Defects in the gelcoat could allow water to penetrate, and even if this is in only minute quantities it may well spread along the hair-like inner strands of the synthetic fibres. This possible penetration of water can result in some major problems later, as a result of inferior or damaged gelcoat.

In reality, a new boat should be trouble-free for some considerable length of time. To keep it so, it should be washed thoroughly with mild detergent and warm water at least once a year. On such occasions, no stubborn stains should be overlooked as there are a number of reliable releasing agents and oil-removing fluids available to assist in their removal. In addition, the removal of minor scratches should also be undertaken. This can usually be done by using a small quantity of rubbing compound, although more stubborn marks may require the careful use of a little 400-grade wet-and-dry paper. In all cases do be careful not to remove too much gelcoat. The annual cleaning should be followed by polishing

all of the fibreglass surfaces with a proprietary fibreglass liquid polisher.

Look After It!

Regular close attention to cleaning and polishing enables the owner to take note of any hairline cracks, scratches or gouges appearing in the surface of the gelcoat. These should not be ignored because they may allow water to penetrate the hull. Booklets giving easy, practical solutions to rectify these more serious problems are available from marine paint manufacturers or your chandler, and another book in this series, *Glass-Fibre Boat Repair*, also goes into the maintenance of GRP in greater detail.

If the hull is suffering from blistering, it could be due to osmotic action. Here it is best to consult an expert to establish the nature and treatment. The same applies with impact fractures – obtain advice first – although most repairs can be undertaken by the boat owner.

Hull Shapes

Now I have examined the various

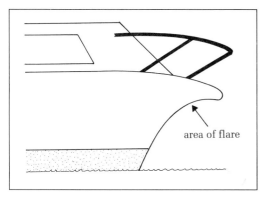

The curvature of the hull at the bow of a boat is called the flare. Many boats have very little flare, but some of the older timber or early glass-fibre types have nicely rounded bows with plenty of flare.

materials that are used in the construction of boats, I will look at the actual shapes of the hull forms and how these shapes affect the performance and economy of the boat in actual cruising conditions.

Where power boats are concerned, there are basically three hull profiles: displacement, semi-displacement and planing. Planing hulls do not generally have a very economical performance at slower, displacement speeds and can also sometimes be difficult to steer and control when below their optimum speed for any length of time, although certain simple modifications can be done to the hull in order to overcome this. If the boat is to be used for high-speed skiing, racing or long-

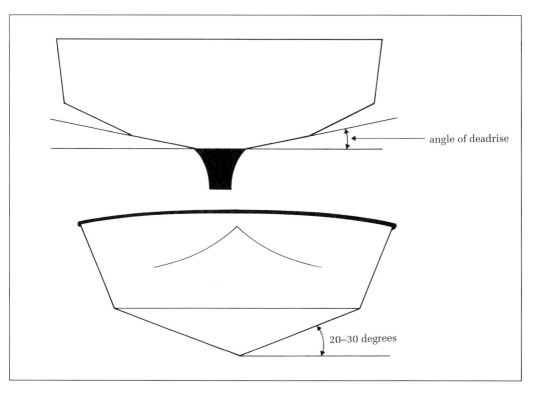

The angle of deadrise determines the type of hull, whether displacement, semi-displacement or planing. An angle of between 20 and 30 degrees usually determines a planing hull.

To help a boat hull perform well in the water, special plates operated by rams can be fitted on the transom below the water-line. Called trim tabs, these can adjust the hull to compensate for uneven distribution of weight, offset fuel and water tanks, and so on.

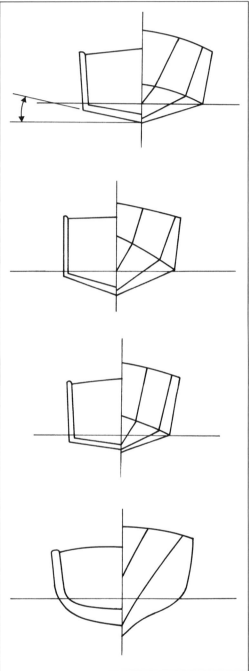

distance cruising, the planing hull with a larger engine will be the best choice. If the boat is to be used mainly at slower, displacement speeds it is probably best to opt for a craft specifically designed with this purpose in mind rather than choose a planing hull when the extra speed capability will be used only occasionally.

Although this book is mainly concerned with seagoing craft and river cruisers, if you are intending to use your boat on the canal system then a flat-bottomed narrow-beam steel-hulled boat will be the best choice. However, the advice given here will apply as much to inland waterway craft as to their coastal cruising counterparts.

Seagoing vessels can be roughly divided into the three categories already mentioned above, namely: displacement,

Various design characteristics of hull forms.

semi-displacement and planing, and each of these is decided by the hull form and designed speed.

Full Displacement

The full-displacement craft is usually heavily built with a rounded bilge hull form. It is designed to travel through the water rather than skim over the surface like its planing cousin. Being heavily built and having smoothly rounded sections, this type of hull does tend to roll more in bad weather but boats of this type are nonetheless exceptionally seaworthy. Hard-chine displacement craft are also built, but they are considered to be full-displacement cruisers because their engine or engines are not powerful enough to push the hull beyond displacement speeds. They do, however, roll less due to

the flat chine sections on the hull which act rather like dampeners on the water.

The maximum speed of a true round-bilge displacement boat is decided by its water-line length and no amount of extra power applied will persuade it to go faster. In fact, over-powering a displacement craft will only cause the stern to sink into the trough between the bow as it tries to climb over the bow wave. The narrow and rounded sections aft do not have sufficient lift to support the stern and, taking an example to the extreme, if unlimited power was available the stern of such a vessel would eventually be forced underwater, causing the craft to sink.

Full-displacement craft, therefore, cannot travel fast but they are extremely economical to run as very little power is required to drive such a boat at anything

The rounded hull form of a full-displacement vessel. This particular boat is shown during building and is made from steel plate.

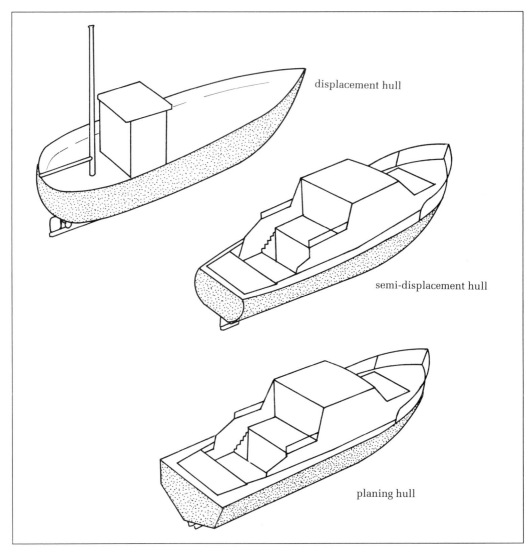

displacement hull

semi-displacement hull

planing hull

Displacement hulls. Many different types of hull are classified in this group, but generally the underwater shapes are well rounded with a narrow stern, which may have a transom or be rounded off like a canoe. (Courtesy of Perkins Engines.)

Semi-displacement hulls. This hull may be similar to a displacement type, but with fuller aft sections, a shallower keel and a wider transom, which give additional buoyancy towards the stern. Semi-displacement hulls are often used for motor cruisers and patrol boats. (Courtesy of Perkins Engines.)

Planing hulls. General characteristics of this type of hull are a wide transom, high beam-to-length ratio, a V-shaped bottom with fairly flat sections towards the aft and very little keel. A chine or fairly sharp corner is often found at the turn of the bilge. Such boats are designed to lift to the surface of the water and plane. (Courtesy of Perkins Engines.)

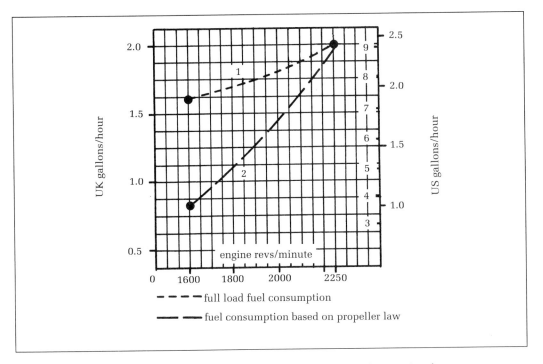

Every marine engine has its own fuel consumption curve. (Courtesy of Perkins Engines.)

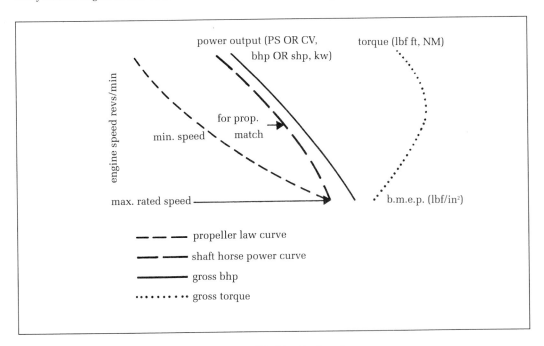

A typical marine engine power curve. (Courtesy of Perkins Engines.)

SPEED AND FUEL CONSUMPTION TABLE				
Water-line length	**Weight (tons)**	**Speed**	**Power required**	**Fuel consumption**
20ft	1.5t	6.5km/hr (4 miles/hr)	8hp	2.27l/hr (4pt/hr)
25ft	5t	7.2km/hr (4.5 miles/hr)	15hp	4l/hr (7pt/hr)
30ft	6t	8km/hr (5 miles/hr)	36hp	9.1l/hr (2gal/hr)
35ft	8t	8.5km/hr (5.3 miles/hr)	40hp	10.2l/hr (2.25gal/hr)
40ft	14t	9km/hr (5.6 miles/hr)	70hp	17.7l/hr (3.9gal/hr)

Note: Consumption figures for petrol engines will be plus approximately twelve per cent.

A comparison of speed to fuel consumption for boats of different lengths, showing the power required to move the craft at a given speed.

below its water-line speed. The longer the boat, the faster it will be, so a large full-displacement cruiser will have a fair cruising speed and economical fuel consumption. The table above will give some idea of the maximum speeds for a given water-line length, the corresponding power required, and approximate diesel fuel consumption needed to attain these speeds. The figures quoted will obviously vary between individual boats, but nevertheless they give a good indication of the fuel economy advantage of a full-displacement craft running at below water-line length speed.

Semi-Displacement

The semi-displacement hull form can also be of round-bilge design, but the underwater sections aft are much wider and flatter than those of the full-displacement cruiser. This large, flat area gives the necessary lift to stop the stern sinking into the trough between the bow and stern waves, and, thus supported, the vessel is able to climb its bow wave and adopt a 'bows-up' attitude as it exceeds its water-line length speed. There is a limit to the speed of this type of craft, this being dictated by the practical consideration of engine size.

The semi-displacement craft is the usual choice of professional seamen for arduous work such as pilot ferrying and harbour patrol duties, where the craft must be capable of going to sea in almost all conditions and still maintain a high cruising speed. The thoroughbreds of the semi-displacement world such as the Nelson range of boats are supremely seaworthy but suffer in the pleasure field from higher running costs than when used for fast cruising full-planing craft.

Planing Hulls

The planing craft has wide, flat sections aft, which are usually joined by lifting rails that run the length of the hull below the water-line. The latter give added hydrodynamic lift, enabling the craft to climb on to the plane more easily and skim over the surface of the water. A fair degree of power is required to lift a boat on to the plane, but once under way the

A stern shot of a semi-displacement hull form. Note the shallow V shape and the 'double hull' which allows the outboard motor to be mounted inboard.

The hull of a fast planing boat. Note the deep V and moulded-in chines. This type of hull is usually found on high-speed sports boats and power craft.

The high-speed inflatable boat. This type of craft is a hybrid, with inflatable sponsons up top and a rigid planing hull form made of GRP below.

power can be eased to give more economical fuel consumption. The latter can be calculated by dividing the total horsepower by twenty to give the consumption in gallons. This will usually give a figure greater than the actual consumption, but it is nevertheless a good method of gauging whether you can actually afford to run the boat. Remember also that once throttled back to cruising revs, the maximum fuel consumption can often be almost halved.

SUMMARY

- The different materials used in the construction of boats have been the subject of continuous development across the centuries, from the simple hollowed-out tree to the sophisticated glass-fibre craft of today.

- Sheet plywood boats usually come in kit form for finishing at home. Confined mainly to smaller craft, such as sailing dinghies and small power boats, this is an ideal way for the DIY boat owner to get himself afloat on a budget.

- The type of boat most commonly seen afloat around coastlines and on inland waterways is made from glass fibre, sometimes called glass-reinforced plastic (or GRP).

- Although this book is mainly concerned with seagoing craft and river cruisers, if you are intending to use your boat on the canal system then a flat-bottomed narrow-beam steel-hulled boat will be the best choice.

4

THE POWER UNIT

The choice of a power unit for your boat is as important a decision as the choice of the boat itself. Careful thought will be required in selecting the engine which, depending upon the type of boat and the use to which it will be put, can amount to a cost not dissimilar to that of the boat itself! The correct matching of the engine to the hull is essential if the maximum fuel economy and performance is to be achieved.

Although engine types do vary from manufacturer to manufacturer, there is little that is different in comparable horsepower ratings or, in general terms, the construction of the basic engine whether it be a diesel or petrol unit (the same is true for outboard motors). The final choice depends upon whether you opt for an inboard, an outboard, an out-drive – where the power from the engine is transferred to the propeller via a special leg fitted on to the transom – or a Z drive, similar to the outdrive. You could also (although at far greater expense) go for a special jet-drive unit. The other main consideration, of course, is how much you can afford.

Outboard Units

If cost is the main consideration and you are looking for an engine for a medium-sized boat – say up to about 30 feet in

The outboard motor is a versatile and reasonably economical way of powering a boat. Unlike the fixed-installation inboard engine, it can be removed from the boat and taken home for servicing or winterizing at the end of the season if required.

length – then you might want to opt for an outboard engine. There are many types available from a vast array of manu-facturers, many of them Japanese. All are engineered to a very high standard and have excellent reliability and perfor-mance built in.

Because the outboard is a self-con-tained power unit it does not suffer from many of the installation problems normally associated with an inboard engine. This is also an obvious cost-saving factor because no exhaust, cooling or special hull strengthening arrangements will be required. Another important consideration (especially on the smaller boat) is space. While an inboard takes up a good deal of room, the outboard is installed either on the transom overhanging the stern of the boat or on to a special beam, enclosed in a 'well' with the lower leg extending into the water below the hull. Smaller outboards also have an integral fuel tank, and even the larger horsepower units have a smaller, perhaps 23-litre (5-gallon) tank attached by a rubber fuel line. This saves the space normally taken up by a large fuel tank – containing over 1,136 litres (250 gallons) – which is the usual installation with a diesel inboard.

Another point of convenience is that you can remove the outboard from the boat to take it home for storage and maintenance over the winter months. If a fault should ever develop, it is also far easier to remove the engine from the boat in order to service it.

If you intend to use an outboard/boat combination for high-speed cruising or a fast activity such as water-skiing then a higher running cost should be expected. An hour's water-skiing at speeds in excess of 40 knots can add considerably to the overall running costs of the boat – especially with fluctuating petrol prices.

Diesel Inboard Units

Inboard engines fuelled either by petrol or

There are many types and sizes of inboard engine – both petrol and diesel – to suit almost all classes of boat. This one from Perkins is a turbo-charged M80T.

diesel come in a wide variety of horse powers to suit most types of boat from 25 feet in length upwards. The standards of engineering are such that today most modern marine diesel inboards and their petrol-driven equivalents offer reliability, durability and economy of use. Where weight and very high speed are of secondary importance in your calculations, fitting an inboard diesel unit would perhaps be your best option.

The diesel engine is an efficient unit with a high compression ratio and has the ability to produce more shaft horsepower from its fuel than almost any other engine. The main drawback is the rather high power-to-weight ratio – the result of the heavy cast block used – although modern castings and computer design methods have produced several lightweight versions.

Outdrive Units

If you intend to install an inboard in a fairly small boat where space is naturally at a premium, it might be worth considering utilizing an outdrive or Z-drive leg which takes up less space. This system is rather like having the best of both worlds: the practicality of an outboard with the security and protection from the weather that an inboard has. The outdrive is a special unit that is close-coupled to the inboard engine and transfers its power from a horizontal plane, through the vertical and back to the horizontal again using special gearing. The advantages of this are that it negates the need for a long propeller shaft and its associated bearings, thus allowing the main power unit to be installed much nearer the stern of the boat.

The outdrive or Z-drive unit is a combination of an inboard and an outboard. Basically, it transfers the drive from the inboard engine from a horizontal plane via the vertical and back to the horizontal again. An advantage of this system is that the propeller can be cranked up for examination or to clear weeds in a similar way to that of an outboard.

The outdrive unit itself incorporates the gearbox, propeller shaft and propeller in one casing which can be manually or hydraulically tilted and lowered into and out of the water. The unit is mounted centrally on the transom of the boat rather like a conventional outboard engine, and the tilt mechanism allows good access to the propeller if, for example, it becomes fouled when underway. Access to the propeller on a standard stern tube arrangement is much more difficult, usually requiring a dive overboard!

Basic Installation of an Inboard Motor

Now that I have gone through the procedure of actually choosing an engine for your new boat or a replacement one for a second-hand model, I will now look at how the power unit is actually fitted into the hull. Initial attention given to the installation of your boat's main source of propulsion – its engine – is paramount in determining its future performance, reliability and operational characteristics. The life of even the finest piece of machinery can be shortened considerably by incorrect installation techniques. Conscientious manufacturers of engines should be able to supply you with copious notes and diagrammatic representations on the step-by-step procedure for installing their products. This not only assists the boat builder or DIY boat owner in installing his engine, but it also protects the manufacturer's reputation.

Before you start your installation, take time out with a pencil, pad and your manuals. Draw a scale plan of your engine compartment and sketch it all out with approximate sizings that can be fine-tuned later. Remember that it is easier to make a cheap mistake on paper at this stage than an expensive one on the boat later when you are half-way through your installation!

You Need Space!

One of the prime requirements when installing any engine is accessibility. An engine that is installed in a cramped and inaccessible engine compartment will be very difficult to service or to access in the event of a breakdown – an important consideration when cruising at sea where the ability to effect even a temporary repair can mean the difference between safety and tragedy. Any installation should also be able to offer easy access to

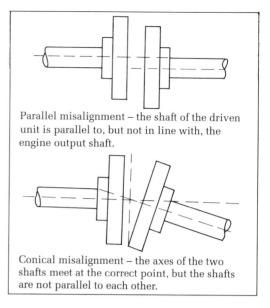

Parallel misalignment – the shaft of the driven unit is parallel to, but not in line with, the engine output shaft.

Conical misalignment – the axes of the two shafts meet at the correct point, but the shafts are not parallel to each other.

The two main problems with shaft misalignment when installing an inboard engine.

'daily check' items such as the oil filler cap, dipstick, water header-tank filler, spark plugs and drive belts, as well as space to check for oil leaks, fuel problems and signs of overheating.

Any routine or end-of-season maintenance should also be possible with the engine *in situ* (outboard motors, covered on pages 64–8, are different, however, as they can usually be taken off the boat and serviced at home), which means that all major components – fuel filters, oil filters, spark plugs, fuel injectors and water pump assemblies – must be accessible. There must also be room for the power unit to be completely removed from the engine bay without having to partially dismantle the boat.

To provide a solid and stable platform free from the troubles of misalignment, the engine must be supported on solid bearers – the engine bed. The bearers may be made of substantial baulks of timber running well into the hull of the boat at the stern, with rigid supports and

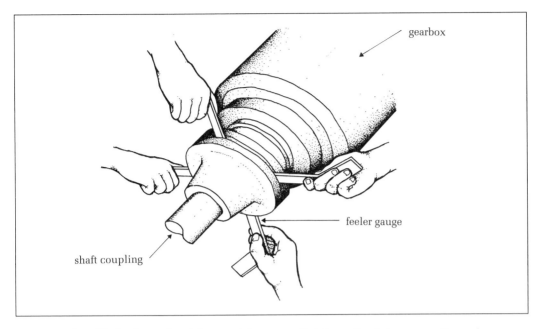

To ensure a long life for the gearbox it is essential to ensure that the mating between coupling and box are within certain tolerances. This is usually achieved with feeler gauges to measure the face run-out.

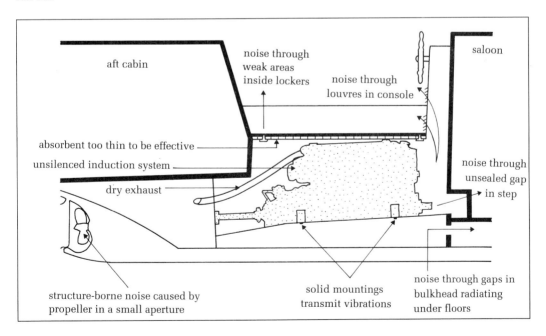

A potentially noisy engine installation.

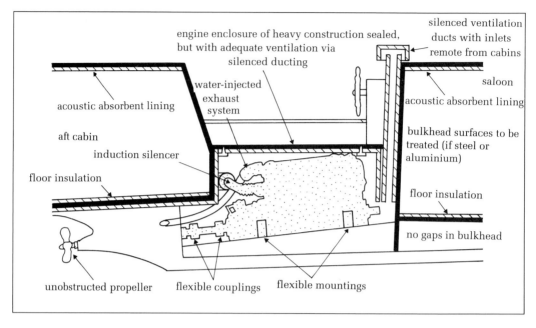

engine enclosure of heavy construction sealed, but with adequate ventilation via silenced ducting

silenced ventilation ducts with inlets remote from cabins

water-injected exhaust system

acoustic absorbent lining

aft cabin

induction silencer

floor insulation

saloon

acoustic absorbent lining

bulkhead surfaces to be treated (if steel or aluminium)

floor insulation

no gaps in bulkhead

unobstructed propeller   flexible couplings   flexible mountings

A quiet engine installation after fitting insulating materials.

strengtheners amidships – including metal strips to prevent the engine feet sinking into the wood. Alternatively,

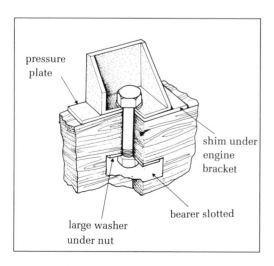

pressure plate

shim under engine bracket

bearer slotted

large washer under nut

Cut-away of an engine mounting foot.

smaller, but obviously stronger steel girders can be secured and glassed into the hull using glass fibre if the hull is GRP, or welded and bolted to the hull if it is steel. All the bearers should extend as far as possible into the boat to help distribute the engine load as evenly as possible. Thrust movements caused by acceleration and deceleration can cause severe forces that will act directly on the main engine bearers, so rigidity is of prime importance.

Engine Mounts

When purchased, most engines come complete with a set of mounting feet, which are as important as the bearers. They can be bought in a variety of sizes and grades of 'softness' depending upon the type of installation required. Most feet are of the

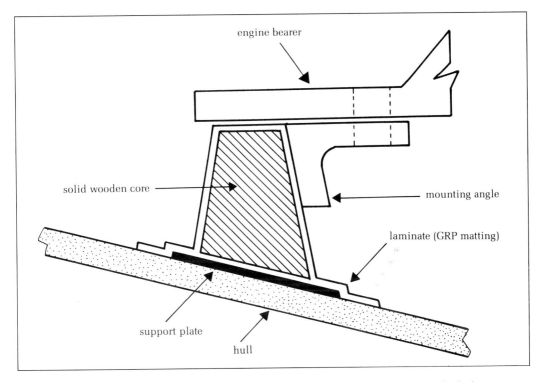

engine bearer

solid wooden core

mounting angle

laminate (GRP matting)

support plate

hull

A timber engine bearer is glassed in using fibre-glass mat and resin. This is a popular method of fitting bearers to a new boat or when replacing older bearers.

bonded-rubber unit variety and come in a range of flexibilities to suit various engine/bearer combinations. Engines that are mounted flexibly are usually quieter and vibrate less than those that are mounted solidly and directly on to the engine beds themselves.

If you use flexible mounting feet, you should remember that all the associated attachments and component parts, such as exhaust pipes, cooling and control linkages, and, even more importantly, the stern tube and its coupling that carries the transmission of power to the propeller, should also have sufficient flexibility to allow for engine movement.

Stern Equipment

The aspect of installation that causes most DIY enthusiasts and even some professional boat builders to break out into a cold sweat is the alignment of the stern equipment – the propeller shaft, the gearbox that transmits the torque from the engine to the shaft, the bearings upon which the shaft will turn and their support brackets. It makes little difference whether the engine is solidly or flexibly mounted; the alignment of the stern gear is still essential in achieving a smooth-running, vibration-free engine installation. It is sometimes thought – incorrectly in my view – that if a flexible

The power output from an inboard engine is transferred to the propeller via a shaft or stern tube joined with special couplings and mounted on bearings.

coupling is used then accurate alignment can go to the wall. This is not so, as shaft and coupling failure and vibration will all be reduced to a minimum if the stern gear is aligned accurately.

The two main types of misalignment that occur can be seen in the diagram on page 52 and are commonly called parallel misalignment and conical misalignment. With parallel misalignment, the output shaft from the engine and the shaft of the drive unit are parallel but not in line with each other; in the case of conical misalignment, the axes of the two shafts meet at the correct point, but the shafts are not parallel. The latter form of misalignment can be checked and rectified by the use of a rotating clock gauge firmly bolted to the flange of the drive unit.

Completely flexible couplings (such as the very popular Aquadrive system) almost eliminate the need for accurate alignment – almost! Comprising two constant velocity joints, the couplings will allow for up to 15 degrees of inaccuracy between the output and drive shafts. As a result, much softer engine mounts can be used. I once saw a Perkins engine installed in a heavy displacement motor boat with an Aquadrive coupling. The silence and vibration-free performance, further reduced by the judicious use of sound-insulating materials in the engine compartment, had to be heard to be believed. The use of such flexible drives is now commonplace, and time has shown that they significantly reduce wear and tear problems associated with harder,

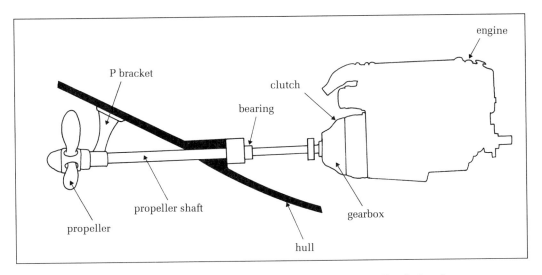

A standard stern-tube arrangement showing engine, gearbox, coupling, propeller shaft and various support bearings.

A range of special Aquadrive flexible mountings from Halyard Marine which allow some flexibility in engine mounting and installation.

non-flexible types of coupling. One boat-yard recently told me that their boats with certain inflexible couplings had a replacement rate of around two per season compared to a nil failure rate with the Aquadrive.

Final adjustments to shafts and couplings should be done with the boat in the water, fully ballasted (if necessary) and loaded as for normal cruising (full water and fuel tanks). Shim washers under the engine feet can be added or taken out as required as the rotation of the shaft and its axis are carefully monitored with clock and feeler gauges. When the correct alignment has been achieved, the shim washers should be measured for their thickness with a micrometer and replaced with solid metal packing plates to exactly the same pattern.

Cooling Systems

The three main methods used for cooling

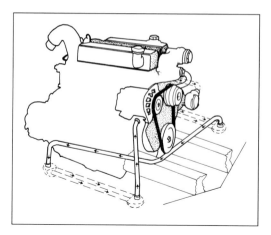

Keel cooling system with twin-keel-pipe circuits. The small keel pipes are built into the keel of the boat during construction. As the boat moves through the water, the sea water cools the engine water. (Courtesy of Perkins Engines.)

inboard engines are: indirect water cooling; direct water cooling; and air cooling. Indirect water cooling uses an internal freshwater system incorporating a heat exchanger. With direct water cooling, the cooling water is fed in 'raw' from the sea or river, filtered, passed around the engine and then dispersed overboard either through the exhaust system or a separate pipe. Air cooling uses a standard fan which blows cold air around the cylinder head and barrel.

When installing an engine, you should consider which type of cooling system you intend to employ. For instance, if you intend the engine to be air-cooled then is there enough ventilation and inlet space in the engine compartment? If you want a raw-water cooling system, are the sea

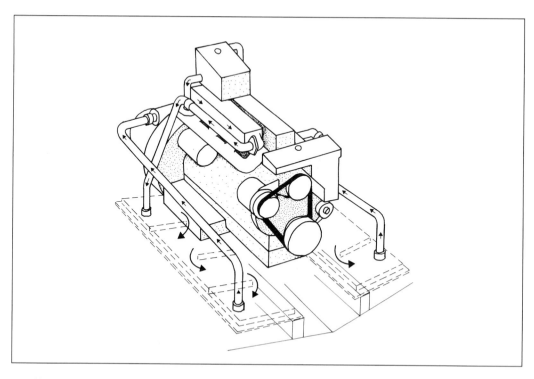

An efficient skin-tank cooling system using two separate circuits. (Courtesy of Perkins Engines.)

cock and pump of sufficient capacity to supply the appropriate amount of water to the engine, and is the straining filter easily accessible? If the cooling system you are going to use is of the sealed-jacket variety with an integral header tank keeping the system topped up, this tank should be mounted above the engine itself where gravity can do its work and the filler cap (which may be pressure rated, depending upon the engine installed) can easily be reached.

All hoses used in the cooling system should have sufficient pressure capability and be secured with strong jubilee-type clips which clamp the end of the hose to the engine outlet pipe. If the engine is to be installed in an open boat and covered with a box, provision should be made for sufficient openings to allow a good flow of air both at the input and output ends of the engine to prevent overheating.

Exhaust Systems

There are two main types of exhaust system for marine engines: wet and dry. With the wet system, water is injected into the exhaust track and dispelled through an exhaust outlet at the stern (usually above the water-line). A 'swan's neck' is usually incorporated into the pipe to prevent any accidental injection of water into the engine itself; this should be fitted with its upper loop high enough to cope with a full loading of the boat. If necessary, a full-flow closing valve should also be fitted into the exhaust pipe.

In a dry exhaust system all exposed pipes should be lagged with fireproof material and routed away from any plastic or flammable materials. Exhausts should not pass through any unventilated areas as this will eventually cause a dangerous

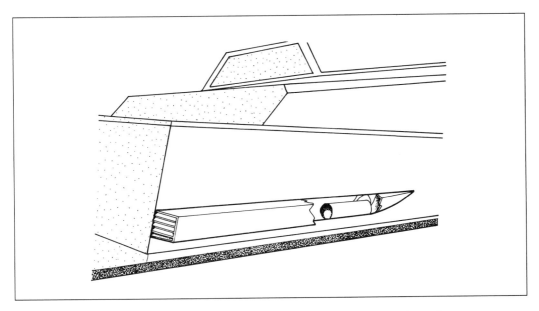

Exhaust channels moulded into the hull sides enable engine gases to be discharged into the slipstream of the boat. (Courtesy of Perkins Engines.)

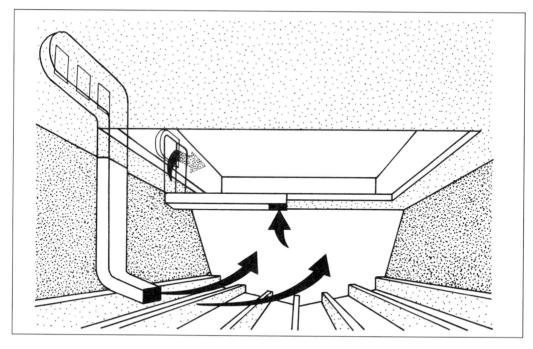

Engine compartment ventilation where ducts on the sides of the hull draw fresh air into the compartment from outside the boat. The stale air is expelled through a forward duct. (Courtesy of Perkins Engines.)

build-up of heat. All pipes should be well supported with brackets and clamps at frequent intervals and should never be twisted or kinked. Exhaust systems should also be easy to access and remove in case of failure or if pipe sections or silencers need to be replaced.

Instruments

The instrumentation fitted to a craft really depends upon the type of engine installed, but the minimum instrumentation on any power unit consists of an oil-pressure gauge, a water-temperature indicator, an ammeter to monitor battery charge, a tachometer to monitor revolutions per minute, and a fuel gauge. Other instruments that may be fitted are an engine hour meter (very useful for determining a maintenance pattern for the engine), gearbox oil-pressure indicator and switches for things such as spotlight, horn and navigation lights. Most modern engines come supplied with a ready-made instrument panel attached to a multicore cable about 3 metres (9 feet) in length. This makes installation much easier for the DIY owner.

The position of the instrument panel in the boat is also important. A console may be used and has the advantage of keeping all the instruments together. It should be fitted within sight of the helmsman so that reflections from the sun off the glass gauges and rainwater accumulation in

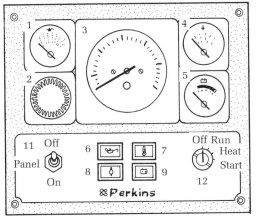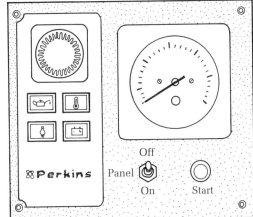

Standard engine instrumentation: 1 engine oil-pressure gauge; 2 audible alarm; 3 tachometer; 4 water-temperature gauge; 5 voltmeter; 6 oil-pressure warning light; 7 water-temperature warning light; 8 oil-temperature warning light; 9 alternator warning light; 10 engine heat/start switch; 11 panel light on/off switch; 12 starter button.

Most engines bought today come complete with a self-contained instrument panel. This is connected to the engine by a wiring loom and a multi-plug and socket, thereby allowing the engine to be removed for major servicing.

bad weather will not affect the instruments or the helmsman's view.

Engine controls should be in a position convenient for the helm, be it tiller or wheel steering, and arranged so that they cannot be knocked or moved accidentally. A single-lever control box is probably best as the engine is placed into automatic idle when the lever is brought to the netural position, without the need to adjust a further lever. The box should be mounted so that when the lever is pushed forward the boat moves forward and vice versa. This sounds obvious, but you would be amazed by the number of people who don't mount it in this way. Good-quality control cables should also be fitted for reliability and peace of mind.

The propeller is the final link in the chain which transfers power from the engine in order to drive the boat through the water.

Propeller Choice

For the optimum performance from any engine/boat installation the choice of propeller is very important. It is the final link in the chain of events and converts the engine power into usable thrust to propel the boat. It is a vital component

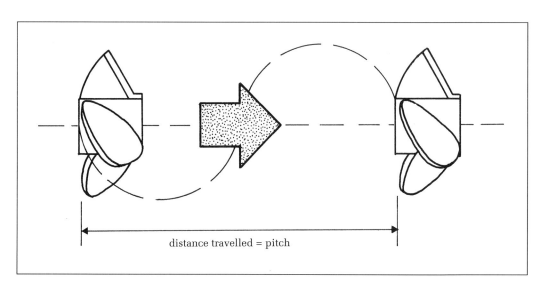

distance travelled = pitch

The pitch of a propeller is the theoretical distance travelled through the water after one revolution, assuming no slip or friction.

that affects engine life, fuel economy and the performance of the boat itself. With many inboard engine installations the type and shape of the hull has quite a bearing on the propeller used, from a physical as well as performance point of view.

The main elements of a propeller (information taken from Perkins Engines *Installation Manual*) are the **diameter**, which is the circle described by the tips of the blades and which should not be greater than 85 per cent of the propeller aperture; the **pitch**, which is a measurement based on the theoretical distance advanced by the propeller for each revolution of the shaft if there were no slip or frictional considerations; the **slip**, which is the difference between theoretical and actual advance per shaft

revolution and usually expressed as a percentage from 15 per cent for high-speed boats to about 65 per cent for sluggish, slow-moving vessels. The **blade area ratio** is the ratio of the total surface area of the blades to the area of the circle swept by the blades. This ratio varies from about 0.40 to 0.70 according to the requirements of the operating conditions. The **disc area ratio** is the same as the blade area ratio except that it is derived from the developed rather than the actual blade surface area. Finally, **thrust** is defined as the total pressure developed by the blades acting on the propeller shaft and causing the foward movement of the boat.

The thrust is greatest when the boat starts to move away at full throttle, and reduces as the boat's speed increases until the resistance of the hull shape equals the

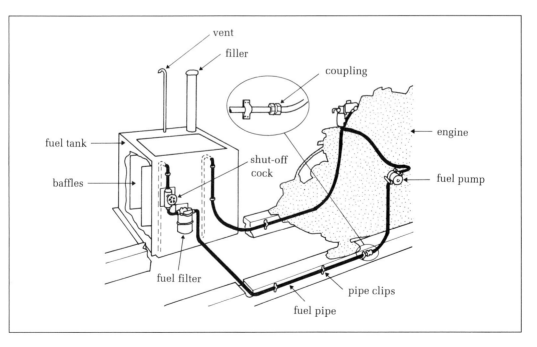

The fuel system of a diesel engine installation showing filter, tank and couplings. (Courtesy of Perkins Engines.)

horizontal component of prop thrust! Sounds complicated, doesn't it? Well, put simply, this means that a propeller with too great a pitch may cause the engine to become overloaded at low speeds whilst one with too little pitch will cause the engine to over-run, causing damage to the prop shaft and, eventually, the engine. Do not be too worried about the choice of propeller. If you are buying a boat from new with an engine already installed, the manufacturer will already have selected the optimum size of propeller for that particular installation. If replacing an old engine with a new or second-hand one, manufacturers' tables and handbooks are available and will give details of the correct prop for any given engine/boat combination depending upon horsepower and conditions of use. The diagrams shown in this chapter give some idea of the make-up and types of propeller commonly used in pleasure craft.

Inboard Summary

It is difficult in a general book about motorboating to cover fully every aspect of inboard engine installation and the lore associated with it. Items such as electrics, fuel and ballasting and trim are all factors to be considered in the installation package. I hope that by covering the main points, first-timers will have a slightly better idea of what is involved. There is no doubt that it is a big job, but it should be within the capabilities of most mechanically minded boat owners.

Do remember to look at the regulations and standards, especially when considering an engine for canal systems or rivers, and do not be afraid to ask for advice from your local boat-yard or engine manufacturer. Remember, it is in

their interests to ensure that you have a trouble-free installation if you are using their products. They would much rather be pestered than have a poor job performed on their engines and stern gear.

Basic Installation of an Outboard Motor

For optimim performance from any boat fitted with an outboard engine, it is essential that boat and motor are suitably matched. This should take into consideration not only the horsepower or power output of the motor, whether short or long shaft, but also the type of hull, length and transom angle of the craft. A motor that is too small for the length of boat will result in slow, sluggish speeds, poor handling and lack of manoeuvrability, whereas one that is too large will cause the boat to be overpowered, hard to handle and prone to capsizing and swamping. Most boat manufacturers specify the maximum horsepower for a particular boat (as do the outboard manufacturers) and it is wise when buying a motor, whether new or second-hand, to follow their criteria. In many cases the power unit is blamed for poor operation when in fact it is the boat and engine match or the installation itself that is at fault.

The Shape of the Hull

A sound, straight and true hull will obviously give the best performance from any given motor installation. However, variations do exist in hulls, especially those made of glass fibre. Distortion of the hull (a problem associated with older boats) forward of the transom area can

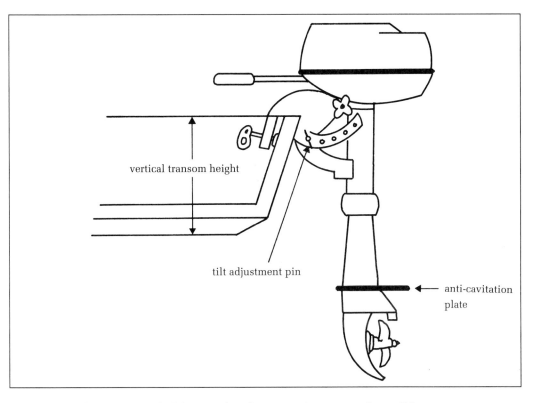

vertical transom height

tilt adjustment pin

anti-cavitation plate

Calculations and mounting method for an outboard motor on the transom of a small boat.

cause a boat's position in the water to fluctuate considerably at speed. Bad curving of the hull will cause a boat to plough through the water, whereas a bulging or convex distortion will cause it to hump or 'porpoise' its way through the waves (*see* diagram right).

The state of the exterior surface of the hull is also very important. A hull covered in barnacles and sea growth is bound to increase drag and will result in a loss of power and poor performance, whereas a smooth, well-polished, maintained and painted hull, treated as necessary with an approved antifouling paint, will eliminate most of the problems associated with a rough-and-ready surface

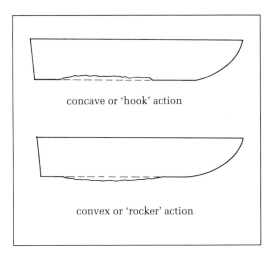

concave or 'hook' action

convex or 'rocker' action

How a misshapen hull could affect the performance of a boat through the water.

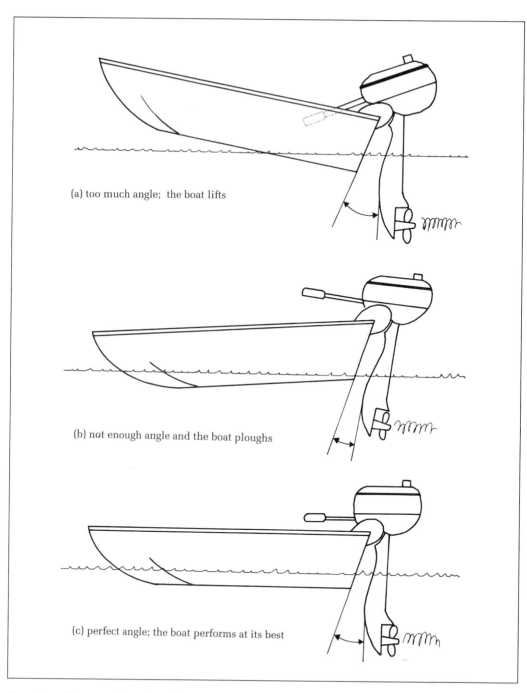

(a) too much angle; the boat lifts

(b) not enough angle and the boat ploughs

(c) perfect angle; the boat performs at its best

An engine with too much angle on the tilt bracket (a) will cause the bow of the boat to lift.
Too little angle between the transom and the vertical outboard leg (b) causes the boat to plough
into the water.
The perfect angle (c) allows both boat and engine to perform at their best.

at speed. Frequent checks on the condition of the painted finish, and the repair and removal of scratches and dents should be carried out.

Transom Angle

The angle of the transom combined with the tilt angles of the outboard should be such that, when the boat is moving the motor is vertical to the water; the thrust from the propeller will then be in line with the direction of travel of the boat. The diagrams on page 66 show what can happen when incorrect tilt angles are employed, as opposed to the correct angle which gives maximum performance and economy.

The outboard will have a built-in tilt mechanism operated either by a mechanical ram, hydraulics (if it is a big engine) or a removable pin-and-notch system that allows for adjustment on most transom angles and conditions of use. However, the correct vertical positioning of the motor can only really be determined when the boat is fully and correctly loaded with the weight aboard evenly distributed. The diagram on page 66 shows a typical transom and outboard, adjusted correctly for maximum operating performance.

Transom Height

The relationship of the transom height to the outboard motor is paramount in ensuring correct propeller depth and in eliminating the problem of cavitation – the creation of a pocket of air in the water around and above the propeller which is caused by the prop itself being too high in the water during operation. A square-ended keel can also cause turbulence that leads to cavitation, but this can be remedied as shown in the diagram below.

Generally speaking, transom height will depend upon whether you buy a short- or long-shaft motor for your boat. Transoms up to 30 centimetres (15 inches) in height (measured vertically from the centre top of the transom to the bottom of the keel or hull) usually require a short-shaft motor, while anything above this measurement

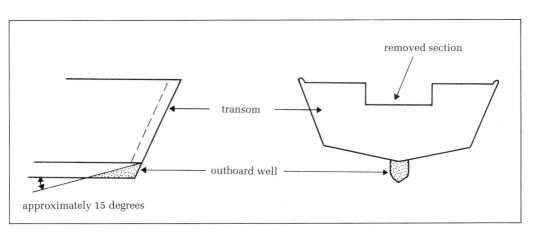

Removing a small portion of the keel right aft could improve the performance of an outboard driven boat. However, consult the manufacturer first!

qualifies for a long shaft. Most outboards are available in both types and a look at manufacturers' literature will give a table specifying transom-to-outboard measurements.

Mounting the Outboard

If you are buying a boat to fit a motor you already own, take a close look at the transom and outboard clamping point – its mount. Remember that this area will have to support the weight of the motor and is also the subject of shock, steering tensions and high-thrust torques. Is it sound?

When you have loaded the engine on to the transom and have centralized it, tighten the clamp screws securely and with even tension to prevent vibration from working them loose; check the tightness of these screws at various times during normal operation. Some transoms are too thick to accommodate a particular motor, in which case they may have to be modified and cut to suit the clamps. Auxiliary outboards – those smaller horsepower units that are sometimes used as a second engine or on sailing boats – are normally fitted on to a fold-down bracket bolted to the transom on the port side to ensure correct steering bias.

Safety Chain

As an extra precaution and to prevent your outboard from sinking like a block of concrete, a safety chain or stout cord should be fitted between the motor and the boat. There is usually a large cast-in ring on the lower casing of the outboard for this purpose. The chain or rope should be long enough to allow easy removal of the engine from the craft on to the mooring pontoon or dry land without having to detach it.

SUMMARY

- Careful thought will be required in selecting the engine which, depending upon the type of boat and the use to which it will be put, can amount to a cost not dissimilar to that of the boat itself!

- Because the outboard is a self-contained power unit it does not suffer from many of the installation problems normally associated with an inboard engine. This is also an obvious cost-saving factor because no exhaust, cooling or special hull strengthening arrangements will be required.

- The diesel engine is an efficient unit with a high compression ratio and is able to produce more shaft horsepower from its fuel than almost any other engine.

- If you intend to install an inboard in a fairly small boat where space is naturally at a premium, it might be worth considering utilizing an outdrive or Z-drive leg which takes up less space.

- One of the prime requirements when installing any engine is accessibility. An engine that is installed in a cramped and inaccessible engine compartment will be very difficult to service or to access in the event of a breakdown – an important consideration when cruising at sea.

5

SECOND-HAND BOATS

Although there are people who will be able to afford to purchase a brand-new boat, many more will probably opt for a nearly new or second-hand craft. The choice of used boats is expansive, with many outlets from classified advertisements in your local paper to the well-stocked marina brokerage pontoons. Even a second-hand boat may be expensive depending upon the model, accommodation, engines and so on, so it is important to prepare yourself with some knowledge of the ins and outs of buying before you part with any money.

A used boat that has had the showroom treatment and is highly polished and

The second-hand boat market is always flourishing. However, do not rush into making your purchase. Take time to examine the boat carefully – even a tatty looking craft can be restored given time and effort.

The deck of this used boat looks awful, but new ropes and a relaid deck covering will alter its appearance considerably.

Minor damage like this to the stern quarter of a GRP cruiser is relatively simple to repair. If there is more extensive damage, ask for the price to be modified.

gleaming under the spotlights looks extremely attractive, with its high-gloss hull and sparkling stainless steel trim. But how much of this is just a cosmetic exercise, a trap into which the unwary customer can easily fall? It is always essential to view the prospective boat dispassionately to ensure that it has all the facilities you require (or room to fit them), and that it is built to a high and seaworthy standard throughout. If this means lifting hatches and removing floorboards to check places that are not immediately on view then so be it; take your time and get the salesman to show you all the spots you want to see. If he is reluctant to uncover bilges and inspection hatches then the boat may not be as good as he would have you believe. This can be disappointing, but it is rather better to discover any shortcomings at this stage. Obviously, the asking price will be a guide to the standard of quality of the finished boat and if a cheaper model is chosen, for whatever reasons, then it would be reasonable to expect slightly less from the craft and its equipment. That said, the repairs may be ones that can be done by the owner once he has taken possession.

A Practical Size

The main pointers to buying a used boat are, first to ensure that it can do everything you ask of it, and second that it can do everything to the standard of comfort and safety you require. The size of boat will often be dictated by the amount of money available, but by going down-market to a perhaps less tidy boat it is often possible to get a much larger boat for the same price.

The number of people who will be sleeping on board regularly may also have some bearing on the size of boat required, but do not be deceived by the statement 'full sleeping accommodation for six' in a 20-foot boat. It is certainly physically possible to sleep six people in reasonable comfort on a 20-footer, but in the morning – when they all want to get up at the same time and use the chemical toilet, and then demand breakfast from the tiny two-burner hob – the real problems become apparent. Twenty feet is the practical minimum size for four people for occasional overnight holidays, but it is more suited to two people for longer breaks.

The smallest of cruisers are often built without a proper toilet compartment. This gives extra living accommodation, with the toilet being located beneath one of the bunks. This is usually acceptable for small families, but it is not really a suitable arrangement for owners wishing to entertain.

The galley needs to be equipped so that it can cater for the maximum number of people likely to come aboard. It must also have sufficient storage space for food and drink for at least a couple of days, with an adequate water supply for both drinking and washing.

On larger craft, where space is not at a premium, more emphasis can be placed on comfort, with separate cabins for guests and additional toilet compartments with built-in showers. In this case the safety aspect of the boat's layout should be studied. Is there easy access from each compartment in case of fire? If the engines are under the floor in the wheelhouse amidships, can the forward and aft cabins be evacuated from an exit other than the wheelhouse doors? The usual method of ensuring that no area of the boat becomes a trap in the event of fire is to fit large opening hatches or windows fore and aft, so remember to check this point. While on the subject of fire, check the number of extinguishers supplied and see if an auto-extinguishing system is fitted to the engine compartment.

Common Sense

Much of the above will also apply to new boats, but with second-hand models you will need to take a much closer look at all the equipment and fittings as well as the general overall condition of the craft. On boats of around 20 feet and below it will probably not be necessary to employ a

Small blisters like this could mean osmosis, or boat pox. It can be cured if not too extensive, but take professional advice and have a survey done first.

marine surveyor to check the boat over as there is less to see and common sense will take care of most problems.

Never buy a boat without seeing it out of the water, however small it is, as the state of the bottom is probably the most important factor to check. Most people have now heard of osmosis which causes the gelcoat below the water-line on GRP boats to blister. Water penetrates the outer surface and forces the gelcoat away from the underlying layers of mat and resin. Once this happens water can begin soaking into the actual lay-up of the boat by 'wicking' along the individual fibres of the mat, thus causing the structure to soften. If left unattended the problem can be unrepairable. If extensive blistering below the water-line is found then either forget the idea of buying the boat or, if the price is very low, employ a surveyor to see whether it would be possible to repair the damage.

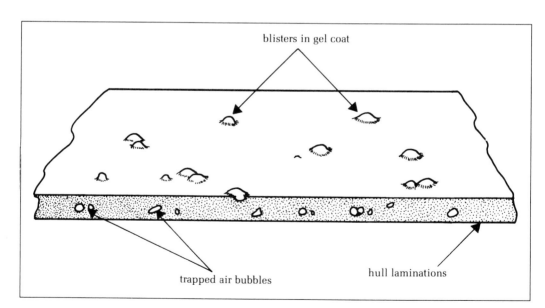

Osmotic blistering shows up as small bubbles in the gelcoat of a glass-fibre boat.

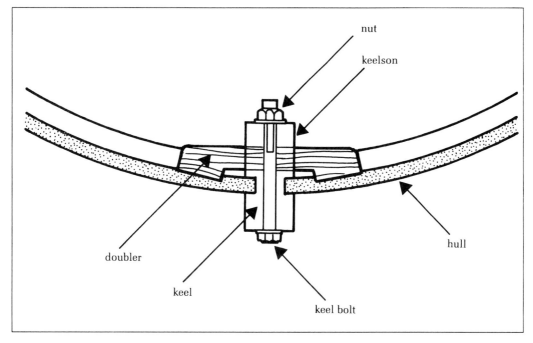

On older boats the keel bolts can suffer from corrosion. Sometimes the only way of telling this is to have them X-rayed – it is expensive, but it is worth it if it saves you money in the long term.

Crazing of the gelcoat is another problem often found on older boats, but this is far less serious than osmotic blistering. It can usually be repaired by removing any loose areas and then filling with an epoxy filler after allowing any dampness to dry out.

Steel and Wood Boats

Steel boats should be checked for signs of corrosion and rust, and wooden boats should be examined for soft areas where rot is setting in. All types of larger craft will be fitted with sacrificial anodes and these should be partly corroded to indicate that they are performing their proper function. If completely wasted away it is possible that corrosion has set in on major pieces of equipment or the hull itself in a steel boat. If they are new-looking they have either been recently fitted or are incorrectly bonded to the hull and items of equipment which they are designed to protect. If painted over they are unable to do their job and have probably been fitted by an owner who does not understand their purpose.

Mechanics

If the overall condition of the exterior is good or reasonable then take a closer look at the stern gear. On outdrives and outboards look for oil leaks and ask to see the condition of the oil in the leg. If it is milky in appearance there has been water penetration into the leg. Although not a valid reason for rejecting the boat, this should mean a reduction in price as the leg will require overhaul of the oil seals and gaskets, and may even need replacement gears if corrosion has set in.

An examination of the condition of the propeller blades will give a good indication of the sort of use the boat has had. If they are chipped and bent the boat may have been run aground at some time, although this may also have been caused if the boat has hit floating debris. Whatever the reason, if the propeller has been in this condition for some time the vibrations which this causes may have damaged internal bearings.

For conventional stern gear the same applies to the propeller as for stern drives, but the condition of bearings can be checked by lifting the prop shaft and checking the amount of movement in the aft bearing. This may be a rubber bearing if fitted in a 'P' or 'A' bracket and allowance should be made for the natural reliance of rubber when checking. If the shaft is located in the keel and there are signs of grease around the aft end, then metal bearings are more likely to be fitted and there should be very little shaft movement. A similar check can be made on the rudder and bearings to estimate the amount of wear that has taken place and the overall condition.

Exteriors

Moving on to the deck, check the firmness of the fittings to see that they have been fitted correctly – in particular, check

When examining a second-hand boat, give the deck fittings a good tug. Loose or damaged ones will show up.

The most vulnerable part of any boat is its canopy. The weather plays havoc with canopies and can soon rip open even a small tear. Canopies can be repaired and the perspex windows replaced, but watch the cost.

cleats, fairleads, grab rails and deck guard-rail stanchions. While walking around the deck, check the effectiveness of the non-slip surface. It may need recoating with a non-slip paint if the present surface is worn.

Cabins

A good indication of the general state of the boat can be obtained by smelling the air as soon as you enter the cabin. If it has a strong musty smell then the first beginnings of rot may be appearing behind wooden panels. If properly ventilated, it should smell fairly fresh and not unduly damp. Have as many floorboards up and look behind as many panels as you can – especially in the bottoms of lockers – to get an idea of how the boat has been looked after. If rot is found in panels or even in the hull of a wooden boat, think very carefully before buying.

Engine Condition

The only way to gauge the actual condition of the engine or engines is to go out in the boat, but a preliminary idea can be obtained by looking at the state of the oil. Diesel engine oil should be jet black, while petrol engine oil is generally a

Always check the engine before buying a boat: ask for it to be run up to temperature and preferably give the boat a test run. This inboard has been left without a bilge pump and rainwater has flooded in and caused damage to the propeller shaft and its couplings.

lighter grey. If any signs of milkiness are found then suspect water in the oil and possible engine damage through corrosion.

Check all the equipment on board for general condition and then ask for an inventory of all the equipment included with the boat so that there are no arguments when the final price is struck. If the boat suits your requirements at this stage and appears to be in reasonable condition, it is either time to make an offer or, if a professional opinion is required, to employ a qualified surveyor to make an in-depth report of the entire craft.

SUMMARY

- The second-hand boat market usually has an excellent selection of many types and varieties of boat, and most people usually find just what they are looking for.

- These days there is almost no fault or repair work that cannot be tackled by the amateur given sufficient time, money and enthusiasm, but care should be taken when considering buying a boat that requires large amounts of work.

- One of the biggest problems facing glass-fibre craft today is that of osmotic blistering. This problem is caused by a variety of means during the construction stage and appears to effect modern boats slightly more than older models.

- One good method of checking the hull visually is to put your eye close to it at one end and scan along the length. This usually shows up any imperfections quite clearly. Another way is to run your hands along the hull – it may be possible to feel any undulations or large areas where repair work may have been carried out.

- If the engine is covered in a film of oil, and pools of water and grime lie under it and over its mounts, you can usually assume that the installation has been badly taken care of.

- The professional marine surveyor will inspect the boat and make a full written report, detailing the condition of all aspects from the hull to the electrical system.

6

SAFETY AFLOAT

What sort of equipment do you need to carry on board the boat? Is it all necessary and would it get you out of trouble if you got into difficulties at sea? These are the questions every potential motor boat owner who intends to take his craft out from the relatively safe confines of the river or canal system should ask himself. Having the attitude 'it will never happen to me' is a very negative one, for one day it surely will. Everyone who takes to the sea is responsible not only for himself, but for the other crew members and also for anyone else present.

The boat owner who ventures out in his boat without any safety equipment, a means of summoning help or the ability to escape his craft and survive in a storm can only be regarded as a fool who is tired of living. The rescue services tell us that many accidents at sea could easily be avoided and that most are the result of badly prepared people crewing badly prepared boats.

Many new boats do not come complete with everything that is essential for a safe sea passage – the consequence no doubt of a policy by boat builders and sellers to keep the price down. A second-hand boat may, however, be much better equipped, with such items as an echo-sounder, a VHF radio-telephone and life-raft having already been installed by the previous owner or owners. If you are a first-time buyer or owner who is thinking about

navigating in tidal waters, you should therefore decide upon the equipment required and make sure that once it has been purchased it goes with you each and every time you set out. You may not be able to afford it all at once, but when compared to the initial cost of the boat, an outlay spent on safety extras and essential equipment is money well spent to make the boat a safe and enjoyable environment in all conditions.

The most important items of a motor boat's equipment are those selected for use in an emergency or to provide safety back-up in time of bad weather, breakdown or accident. Basically, safety equipment can be divided into two sections: general safety equipment, which includes a life-raft, flare pack, first-aid kit and so on; and personal safety equipment, which might include a life-jacket, buoyancy aid, whistle, strobe light, EPIRB (Electronic Position Indicating Radio Beacon) and hand-held VHF radio.

Life-Raft

Every motor boat over approximately 30 feet in length should have a serviceable life-raft aboard. They come in many shapes and types, from simple, open, inflatable boats to the more complex (and expensive) automatically inflating rafts. The latter come complete with a pro-

The VHF radio is an essential item aboard any motor boat. It is far quicker and probably more successful when calling for help in times of emergency.

A life-raft is usually only carried on larger boats that make regular sea voyages. Modern rafts have built-in shelter and emergency survival rations, and self-inflate on hitting the water.

tective seaproof hood, life rations, flares, a small cooker, the means of making fresh water from the sea and automatic beacons which will bleep out the exact position fix by satellite and which are activated as soon as the life-raft hits the water. With such a variety of rafts and boats to choose from, the price you pay will also vary considerably. Remember, though, that a life raft could well provide the only means of escape from a sinking or burning boat, so buy the best that you can afford.

Flare Packs

Flares are another obvious item to have on board and these, along with the VHF, are usually an excellent means of summoning or attracting help. Some companies can supply flares both individually or in special all-in packs. They will even advise individuals on the best selection of flares for their particular type of boat and area of use.

Probably the most effective flare is the red parachute rocket which can be fired to a height of around 300 metres (1,000 feet) and which will burn a brilliant red colour for around forty seconds. Boats that regularly go to sea should have at least five such flares, supplemented if possible by

An EPIRB (Emergency Position-Indicating Radio Beacon) is a useful addition to the boat's safety equipment. When activated it gives off a wide-ranging radio signal that can be picked up by the emergency services who use it to get a fix on the vessel in trouble.

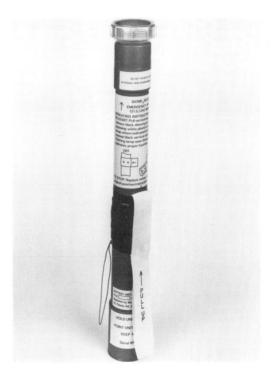

Flares are another good way of raising help and indicating the position of a boat in trouble.

two or three red hand-held flares for close observation. Orange smoke is another useful device to have on board, but note that the white rockets that are available are used mainly to pinpoint a craft's position and are not usually used in distress circumstances.

The flare pack should be stored in a cool, dry place, near at hand (a cupboard near the helm is ideal) and should be removed from the boat during the winter months. Most flares come in waterproof packs and are clearly labelled. They also have a shelf-life and should be replaced when this date is exceeded.

Life-belts, Life-lines and Life-Jackets

There should be at least two life-belts or buoys positioned at both ends of the boat on easy-release hooks for use in man overboard rescue. These can be of the circular or horseshoe type and should ideally have a strobe flasher or light and whistle fitted to make location in the dark or fog that much easier. Another useful item is a length – approximately 25 metres (80 feet) – of life-line attached to each of the buoys, or a rubber quoit (ring) attached to its own length of nylon cord to act as a useful hand-hold in rough conditions. Make sure the life-lines are of man-made fibre as in the majority of cases this will float; a brightly coloured line is also useful.

You should provide each member of your crew with a BSI approved life-jacket – these types are not completely dependent upon mouth inflation and have an automatic CO_2 device which blows the jacket up as soon as it hits the water. As with life-belts, these should also have a strobe flasher and a whistle attached to a short lanyard.

Life-jackets and/or buoyancy aids should be provided for every member of the crew. Ensure that children know how to put theirs on quickly and without panic.

Fire Prevention

Fire is always a worry at sea, so preventative measures should be taken at all times. This is where crew training is essential, but it should always be backed up with the correct equipment for dealing with the different types of fire should one start.

At least two fire extinguishers should be fitted; both should be of the readily available, dry powder type which usually comes in sizes up to 3 kilograms (6½ pounds) for smaller boats. Alternatives are CO_2 or foam extinguishers. They must be checked regularly for capacity and for

Fire extinguishers are another essential safety item. Make sure that your boat is equipped with the right number of the correct type. The engine compartment can be fitted with a halon-gas system for extra protection.

flames. A plentiful supply of water will obviously be available, so two buckets with long lines can be a help when extinguishing wood and fabric fires. However, never pour water on to an electrical fire and take extra care when gas is involved.

More sophisticated extinguishing systems are available for the engine compartment. They operate in a similar way to water sprinklers in buildings: a bulb of wax melts to set off halon gas under pressure. This sort of system is being fitted as standard in many production boats. It can be expensive, but as it is very efficient it may be well worth the extra cost.

Anchors and Pumps

Every boat that goes to sea should have an anchor of a suitable size and weight, which should be shackled securely to a length of chain and warp (rope) of an appropriate length for the boat and likely cruising grounds. Many craft have a special locker in the bows for storing the anchor warp, leaving the 'hook' itself to be stored on deck near the bows. Accidents can be prevented by clipping the anchor in place, but it should always be ready for action.

A good general-purpose anchor that will hold in most ground situations is the Bruce which can be bought in several sizes. For a boat of about 30 feet in length an anchor of 12 kilograms (26 pounds) would suffice.

A good-quality bilge pump should be fitted in the lowest accessible point of the bilges and worked either automatically through a float switch or by hand. This can be backed up by a small hand pump if required.

the correct operation of the firing mechanism. A label on the side of each extinguisher will give a date for the next service. The extinguishers should be positioned in the galley, main saloon, engine room and helm. In larger cruisers with separate cabins it is a good idea to fit an extinguisher in each one for extra peace of mind. The galley – a place where many fires start on board – should, in addition, have a fire blanket installed within reach of the cooker. A small bag of sand is also useful for containing any

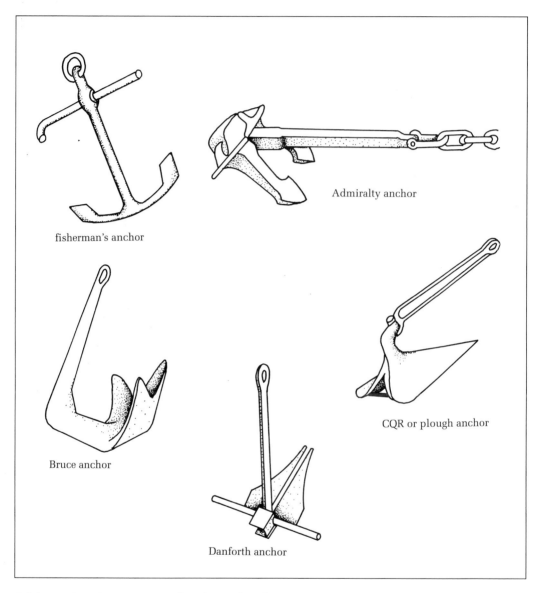

fisherman's anchor

Admiralty anchor

Bruce anchor

CQR or plough anchor

Danforth anchor

A fisherman's anchor. Everyone's idea of an anchor, these are now rarely used on modern motor boats.

The Admiralty anchor. Used by the Navy (hence the name), these are hardly ever seen on board the pleasure boat.

The Bruce anchor. A useful anchor designed for a variety of holding grounds, from rocks to mud and sand.

The CQR or plough anchor. It is good for sand, mud and weed, but is not very effective on rocky bottoms.

The Danforth anchor. This anchor is excellent on most types of holding ground and is seen on many pleasure boats as well as a good number of commercial craft.

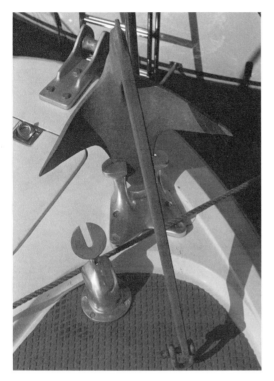

Although not immediately obvious, the anchor also comes under the banner of safety equipment. It is the only means of stopping the boat should the engine fail at sea or in tidal waters.

Charts and Compasses

You should take along charts which cover the areas you intend to cruise: one large-scale chart showing the entire area, and several small-scale ones for harbour entrances and shore cruising will suffice. Store them in a plastic wallet in a dry place along with your other navigational instruments and pencils. Basic chartwork is covered in greater detail in Chapter 7 (*see* page 96).

Your boat should be fitted with a good-quality compass – ideally an illuminated binnacle compass positioned at the helm

and backed up with a hand-held model. Remember, too, that the boat should be fitted with a full set of navigation lights: red to port, green to starboard, a white riding light and a white anchor light. There are many different types from which to choose, but select carefully and fit them in the correct positions. The Royal Yachting Association (RYA) produces a leaflet showing light positions.

In addition to your chart and pilot information, nautical almanacs such as those published annually by Reeds or McMillans give much useful information on tides, harbour plans and town descriptions.

Deck Stores

DECK STORES
Spares for the engine
● Gaskets
● Belts
● Water pump
● Thermostat units
GRP pack
● Resin
● Bonder
● Matting
● Wire
● Hardboard (for formers)
Spares for the inflatable
● Patching kit
● Spare bulbs for the navigation lights
● Torch
Other items
● Aerosols for the hand horn
● Split pins, screws and bolts
● A D-shackle
● Whipping twine
● Thimbles

Deck stores can be described as all the various bits and pieces you carry to enable you to effect a repair, however temporary, on the boat or part of its fabric. The list given in the table on page 83 is by no means comprehensive, but it will get you started with the basics. You will think of many other things to take with you as you go along.

Tool Kit

Tools should be taken aboard to help you cope with GRP maintenance, engine repairs, carpentry and general jobs. Comprehensive tool kits such as the floating Heyco type shown in the photograph (right) are readily available. These contain a variety of spanners and socket-box nuts, along with screwdrivers, saws and wrenches. The best advice when it comes to selecting a tool kit is to buy the best you can afford, and then look after it properly. The amateur DIY owner will be able to do a much better job with a good-quality tool than with one that is poorly made. As a guide, the table below, lists tools and accessories that would make a kit suitable to take on board an offshore cruiser.

The VHF Radio

Apart from the compass and charts

A hand-operated bilge pump can be useful for removing water shipped during cruising, or for pumping out the bilges in case of flooding.

Each crew member should be kitted out fully with protective clothing in case of poor weather.

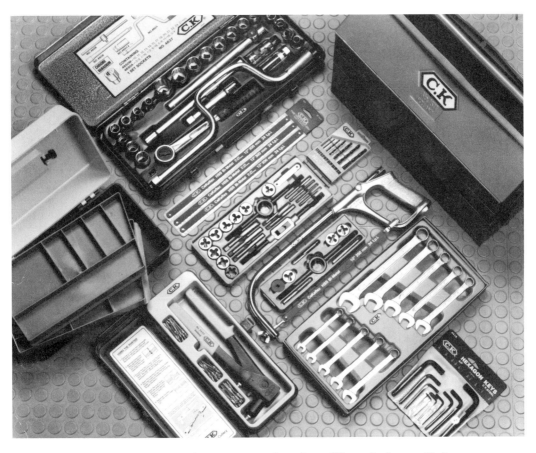

An extensive tool kit should be carried on every motor boat that will be cruised at sea. Tools should be available for engine servicing as well as for repairs to the electrical and other on-board systems.

ON-BOARD TOOL-KIT

- Hacksaw with blades
- Hammer
- Pliers
- Spanners for the engine
- Adjustable wrench
- Mole grips
- Wire brush
- Hand drill
- Assorted twist drills
- Cold chisel
- Padsaw with spare blade
- Soldering iron with solder (12 volt)
- Combination wood saw
- Wire cutter
- Workshop vice mounted on blockboard
- Several files – round and flat, coarse and fine
- Screwdrivers (both types)
- Big wrench

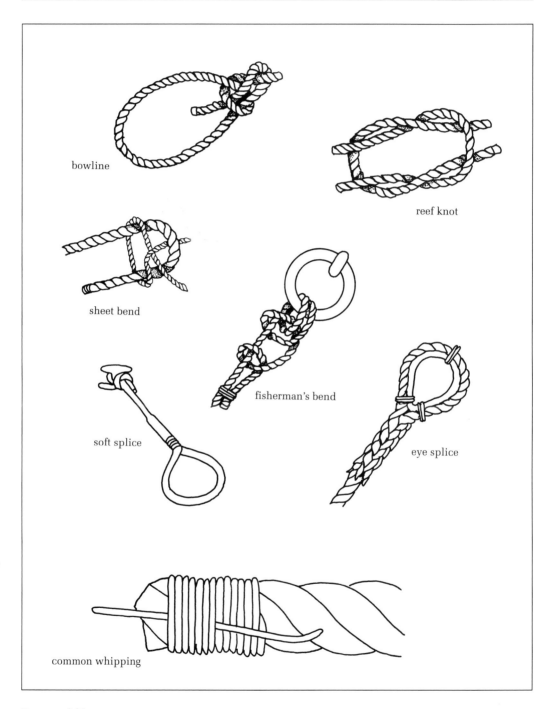

bowline

reef knot

sheet bend

fisherman's bend

soft splice

eye splice

common whipping

Some useful knots.

already mentioned, there are other pieces of navigational gear which, when fitted to the boat, will increase your safety margin. The most obvious item is a VHF radio-telephone, the uses of which are many, ranging from simple ship-to-ship communication to a means of consulting the coastguard, marina or other rescue service. Information can also be received in the form of weather forecasts, storm warnings and other ships' movements.

One of the best types of VHF radio to buy as a permanent installation is a multi-channelled synthesized one, of which there are several on the market. The unit should have Channel 16 facility with an automatic priority and Channel M, the marina frequency. Make sure it is installed correctly and that your propagating aerial is the best you can obtain. As an extra precaution, and if funds allow, a hand-held portable VHF is very handy. It provides means of contacting the rescue services if you are unfortunate enough to have to abandon your boat.

Once your VHF is installed it is essential that you know how to use it proficiently and with the correct terminology. The following sections will give you the basics and can be used as revision rules for your VHF Operator's Licence, an essential item which you will need to obtain before you can use your set legally. It should be remembered that by its very nature the frequency band used for marine VHF is a crowded medium, and that the rules existing for the operation of a set have been created to ensure minimum congestion and maximum intelligibility.

There are three main groups of frequency allocated for special function: intership communication; public correspondence, which is for talking to coastal stations and for link calls to the land-based telephone network; and port operations which include calls to harbour authorities, tug facilities and so on.

Channel 16 – Call and Distress

The most important channel, with priority over all others, is the Call and Distress channel – Channel 16 – and an understanding of its use and operation is essential.

The Call and Distress channel has been established to eliminate the confusion and chaos that would otherwise arise in an emergency situation. If it did not exist, a vessel would have to attempt to contact vessels on any one of the other fifty-seven frequencies available – imagine trying to summon help by switching from one channel to another and repeating your Mayday message over and over again in the vain hope that someone is listening. Channel 16 was therefore introduced and designated a Listening or Call and Distress channel. All main coast stations monitor the frequency twenty-four hours a day every day, and all ships also keep a listening watch. So, if you need to call another vessel, a coastal station, the coastguard or the marina you only need to monitor and use Channel 16. Once contact has been established, both parties then select another working channel by mutual agreement. Normal conversation should never be carried out on Channel 16.

Because of the widespread monitoring of Channel 16, it is obvious that this is the best channel on which to broadcast your call for help. Distress calls should always be made on Channel 16 using the correct procedures and terminology. The Royal

Yachting Association booklet *G22* lists the correct methods for the use of this frequency and the variations for different types of vessel. A call on Channel 16 and the use of the word 'Mayday' indicates that a vessel is in grave danger and requires immediate help. The Mayday procedure is simple:

'Mayday, Mayday, Mayday. This is *Righteous Indignation, Righteous Indignation, Righteous Indignation.* Mayday *Righteous Indignation.* My position is [give latitude and longitude or true bearing and distance from a charted point, and the nature of distress – on fire, aground and so on] Over.'

This call takes priority over all other traffic and imposes a general radio silence. If there is no response, check that the radio is switched on, that power is connected and that the aerial is correctly rigged (this sounds stupid, but it has been known to happen), then repeat the call. If a ship or land base is listening you can expect an immediate answer. If not, repeat several times and then, if necessary, try another channel. Any other channel may be used to transmit a Mayday call.

'Securite' is the word that is used mainly by coastal stations to herald the broadcast of a general navigational warning – for example, a gale warning, a buoy that has dragged its station, an extinguished beacon or a vessel adrift. The initial announcement is made on Channel 16 and an instruction is then given by the coastal station for the skipper to select the channel. When this has been done, the full message and information is broadcast.

The words 'Pan Pan' are used for lesser emergencies where a Mayday call is not necessary; this is also broadcast on Channel 16. It is usually employed when a vessel needs to make an Urgency Call regarding the safety of its crew or the ship itself. An Urgency Call is broadcast in the same way as the Mayday procedure except that the words Pan-Pan are substituted for Mayday.

It may sometimes be prudent to monitor both Channel 16 and the local marina or port frequency, and some VHF radios incorporate a dual watch facility comprising special circuitry that automatically switches between the two channels. When a transmission comes through on one or other of these monitored frequencies, the radio locks on to that particular channel while still retaining priority for Channel 16. This eliminates the need to monitor and determine which channel is carrying the message.

Licence and Certification

Once you have bought a VHF radio you have to licence it. The documents required are a Ship's Licence and a Certificate of Competence in Radiotelephony or an Operator's Licence. To get your certificate you must first sit a relatively easy exam which is usually monitored by the RYA and which takes about one hour. It consists of a written paper of some fifteen questions which is followed by a practical operator's test on a VHF simulator. The full syllabus and a selection of test questions is available in a special booklet from the RYA called *G26*. Once the examination has been passed, the user is then entitled to operate a VHF ship's radio-telephone on any British ship in any part of the world for the rest of his life. It is illegal not to hold such a certificate. The examinations are usually held at the main boat shows such as the London International show in Earls Court during January, the East Coast Show at Ipswich in May and the Southampton Boat Show held at Mayflower Park during September. You may also be able to sit an exam at your local RYA evening class.

The radio itself must also be licensed. An application form will usually be supplied by the dealer who sold you the set, but if it is not you should write to the Department of Trade and Industry. It is renewable on an annual basis and must be kept on board the boat for inspection if necessary. If you cannot produce your licence, your set may be confiscated.

Echo-Sounder

For the close shore cruiser an echo-sounder is another useful item which will help you to navigate a complex channel safely or locate a good anchorage. Once again there are lots to choose from, and several good examples are available at a reasonable price. They are usually the spinning LED types, but with the cost of microprocessors reducing all the time, digital depth-sounders will soon also be inexpensive.

Other navigation units you could fit include radar, more complex radios, sat nav and weather facsimile machines, but these are hardly required by the short voyage, offshore cruising man and there can be a tendency for some boats owners to go wild when buying gadgets!

Clothing

Every crew member should have his own set of oilskins or waterproof clothing, one pair of quality sea boots or wellingtons, gloves, and a covering for the head – preferably a woollen hat which can be supplemented in inclement weather by the hood of an oilskin jacket. Even on short trips a complete change of clothing should be taken along, with a couple of thick jumpers, socks and trousers in case the weather turns nasty.

Deck shoes with rubberized soles should be worn at all times when weather permits; they not only protect the decks and fabric of the boat but help prevent slipping on wet surfaces. Clothes should be kept together on short voyages in a nylon kit bag in the cabin or saloon out of the wet.

Food and Drink

Finally, before setting off check that you have stocked the larder. Food and drink are as important on a cruise – however short – as the boat's engine, and you should never set out without some form of sustenance.

Water is probably the most important item, so keep a couple of gallons of drinking water in a container. A brief trip could see you supplied with sandwiches and biscuits, but add to these some barley sugar sweets and chocolate or mint cake for nourishment just in case you get stranded somewhere. More substantial meals cooked in the galley are, of course, left to individual preferences, but on cold days a large food jar or thermos filled with soup or stew will keep the crew happy and warm whether on watch or at the helm.

ON-BOARD FIRST-AID KIT

- Sticking plasters
- Sterile dressings, with non-adhesive dressings
- Sterile cotton wool
- Elastic bandages
- Triangular bandage
- Adhesive tape
- Scissors
- Antiseptic solution
- Safety pins
- Tweezers
- Pain killers and vinegar
- Foil space-blanket or wool blanket
- Antihistamine cream

Basic First Aid

It is appropriate in this chapter to look at some basic first-aid techniques which should be learned by anyone who is considering buying a boat for the first time, or for those who already own a boat but who want to brush up on their first-aid knowledge. The techniques described below will be of use in all forms of boating, from offshore and coastal cruising to pottering about on rivers, lakes and canals.

General Points

The aim of first aid in an emergency situation is to assess the situation quickly, preserve life when necessary, aid recovery, prevent the deterioration of the victim's condition, protect from further injury and make the victim as comfortable as possible until medical help arrives. It is also the job of those applying first aid to reassure victims and, if necessary, their family or friends.

Although much of first aid is common sense, it is always advisable to have a person present who has a knowledge of first-aid procedures. Short courses are available from organizations such as the St John Ambulance Association.

First-Aid Kit

The first-aid kit is a very important item and should be checked regularly and replenished as necessary; without it you could be in serious trouble with cuts, burns, scalds and sprains. The kit should be stored in a dry plastic box and fitted in a prominent position in the main saloon. The items listed in the table below should be sufficient for short coastal trips, but for longer voyages lasting several weeks or months, and especially those in foreign waters, a more comprehensive first-aid kit will be required. It might be prudent to seek advice from your doctor or pharmacist on exactly what is needed.

Minor Injuries

Small cuts and grazes In the case of minor cuts and grazes the area should be cleaned with antiseptic solution and a sticking plaster applied when necessary.

Stings In the case of a jellyfish sting, apply vinegar to the area as this should counteract the effects of the sting. It is not advisable to attempt to remove any fragments of tentacles with your fingers as you may also be stung; instead, use adhesive tape or a sticking plaster for this purpose. You may also like to give the victim some pain-killers as stings from some species can be extremely painful.

In the case of insect stings, do not try to remove the sting with tweezers as this could burst the poison sac and cause more of the poison to enter the wound. Instead, use a pin, needle or knife blade. The area may then be washed with soap and water, and antihistamine cream applied.

Removal of a fish hook Due to the barb at the end of a fish hook, it is not always possible to pull the hook out backwards. The only way therefore (although it will hurt) is to cut off the end of the hook opposite the barb and continue to push the hook out in the same direction as it entered. Once this has been done the wound should be washed with antiseptic and a dry dressing applied. If the victim has not had a tetanus injection within the past year, you should take him to hospital as soon as possible, preferably on the same day.

Removal of foreign bodies in the eye To remove a foreign body from the eye, first attempt to dislodge the object by flushing clean water across the eye. If this fails, grasp the upper eyelashes and pull the lid out and down. Alternatively, place a matchstick above the upper eyelid and fold the lid back over it to expose the inside of the lid. You may then attempt to remove the object with the dampened corner of a tissue or clean cloth. If these actions do not succeed, seek medical help. Do *not* try to remove any object which is embedded in the surface of the eye as you may cause damage to the cornea.

Nosebleeds Sit the victim comfortably with his head tilted slightly forward and advise him to breathe through his mouth. Pinch the lower nostrils firmly for about fifteen minutes, then release them slowly and ask the victim to refrain from sniffing or blowing through his nose. Any nosebleed that persists after these measures have been taken should be treated at a hospital.

Fainting If a person feels faint, loss of consciousness can sometimes be prevented from occurring if the victim is made to sit in a chair with the head forwards between the knees, thus increasing the flow of blood to the brain.

If the person loses consciousness but is breathing normally, loosen any restrictive clothing and elevate the legs slightly so that they are above the level of the chest. If consciousness does not return with minutes, put the victim into the recovery position and seek medical help. Do *not* leave the person alone. Cover him with a blanket and observe the breathing and skin colour. *Never* attempt to give an unconscious or newly conscious person a drink as this could lead to choking.

Sprains and strains If either of these is sustained, help the person into a comfortable position and elevate the injured part of the body. Apply a cold compress to the area for approximately half an hour to reduce the swelling and ease the pain. Apply an elastic bandage and encourage the victim to rest until medical help is reached.

Seasickness Many remedies are available for preventing this condition and they usually need to be started prior to any trip. When seasickness occurs, encourage the person to rest as much as possible and keep warm. Try to replace lost fluids by offering sips of water. When possible, dry biscuits or bread can prevent the build-up of acid in the stomach. It is never advisable for sufferers to vomit over the edge of a boat as the body is weak and off balance in this state, thus increasing the risk of their falling overboard.

Major Emergencies

In major emergency situations the following principles must be applied when assessing the situation. These points should be remembered in all of the following incidents.

Bleeding Any bleeding should be controlled by applying firm pressure to the wound.

Breathing difficulties Check that the airway is clear of any foreign bodies and that the victim is breathing regularly. When appropriate, put the victim in the recovery position to ensure a clear airway. If breathing has stopped, artificial respiration and cardio-pulmonary resuscitation will have to be commenced – see tables below.

Circulation Problems Check that there is a strong pulse and that the skin is a normal colour. If no heartbeat or pulse can be detected, cardio-pulmonary

---

PERFORMING ARTIFICIAL RESPIRATION

- Lie victim on his back on a firm surface (for example, the deck of the boat), and extend the head by tilting the forehead backwards and the chin upward.
- Remove any obstructions such as dentures.
- Use your thumb and finger to pinch the nostrils together.
- Take a deep breath and place your lips firmly around the mouth of the victim.
- Blow air into the victim's lungs. The first two breaths should be completed in five to eight seconds, and each inflation should take between one-and-a-half to two seconds to complete. Breathe gently, watching for the rise and fall of the patient's chest.
- Turn your head towards the chest to watch the victim's chest fall and listen for the air leaving his mouth.
- Repeat this procedure until the victim is breathing normally, then place the person in the recovery position and cover with a blanket until a hospital is reached.

---

resuscitation (cardiac massage) should be performed, see table. Ideally, cardiac massage and artificial respiration should be carried out by two people simultaneously. However, if there is only one rescuer then about fifteen chest compressions should be applied, alternated with two breaths into the lungs.

Rate of air during Artificial Respiration
Although the air blown into the casualty's lungs by the rescuer only contains about 16% oxygen compared to the 21% in the atmosphere, this should be quite enough to keep the casualty alive.

PERFORMING CARDIO-PULMONARY RESUSCITATION

- Place the heel of one hand over the other on the lower breastbone in the centre of the chest away from the ribs.
- Compress the lower breastbone at a rate of about eighty compressions per minute.
- Continue this procedure until the heart begins to beat spontaneously, or until medical help arrives.

Sunstroke or heatstroke This is a potentially life-threatening condition in which the body's temperature-regulating mechanism ceases to function and the person literally overheats. The signs are headaches, vomiting, dizziness, fainting, rapid breathing, and red and hot skin. Loss of consciousness can follow.

The first-aid treatment for sunstroke is to reduce the temperature of the body by removing clothes from the person and wrapping him in cold, wet sheets, or alternatively sponging the body with cool water. Move the victim away from the sun into a shady place where possible and fan him with a book or magazine. This is an emergency situation and medical help should be sought immediately. If the victim is unconscious then lie him in the recovery position and apply observations as previously mentioned with regards airway and circulation.

Drowning Presuming a life-jacket is worn, if a person falls into the water and is unable to swim to safety, he should be thrown a life-ring or other buoyant object. A rope or a line should be extended towards the victim to enable him to be pulled to safety. Alternatively, where possible, the person should be approached in a boat and pulled to safety by the crew themselves.

Once the victim is aboard, assess his condition and, when necessary, commence artificial respiration and/or cardiac massage. Once the victim is breathing and has a normal heartbeat, place him in the recovery position and keep him warm under a blanket. Do not offer the victim drinks and take him to hospital as soon as possible.

Electric shocks The first action that should be taken in these cases is to remove the victim from the source of electric current. Do *not* touch the person until this has been achieved or you may also receive a shock. If necessary, use another object – for example, a stick – to move the body away from contact with electricity. Do *not* touch the victim with anything that is wet.

If breathing has stopped start the resuscitation procedure as described above. Place the victim in the recovery position, cover with a blanket and get him to hospital immediately; treat any burned area as outlined below.

Minor burns Either immerse the affected part of the body in cold, clean water or hold it under cold running water. Salt water will suffice if it is all that is available, but it will be painful. This immersion will remove any corrosive substance, reduce the heat to the area and help to ease the pain. Remove or undo any restrictive clothing or jewellery and apply a sterile, dry, non-fluffy dressing to the area.

Major burns If the victim's clothing is on fire either roll them in a blanket to put out the flames, or throw cold water over the victim. Do *not* try to remove any clothes that are stuck to the burned area, but instead cover any burned area with dry, clean, sterile (if possible) cloth and secure with a bandage until medical help arrives. Keep the victim warm and comfortable, give reassurance and observe their general condition for signs of shock.

When treating burns, do *not* use adhesive dressings or fluffy substances such as cotton wool as these will stick to the wound. Do *not* apply any creams, lotions, oils or grease, and do *not* try to prick any blisters that may form or interfere with the burned skin in any way.

Fractures A fracture may be suspected following an injury if an area of the body is painful (especially in movement), swollen and tender; in some cases the limb is obviously deformed.

If the arm is injured, make a sling and immobilize the limb across the chest. If a foot or leg is fractured, try to tie the injured leg to the other to act as a splint, or alternatively use an oar or paddle. Place padding between the splint and the limb to prevent rubbing.

A broken finger can be bound to the next in order to immobilize it. In the case of an open fracture (where the bone protrudes from the skin), protect the open wound with a sterile pad and gently bandage in place. Any bleeding should be controlled by applying pressure to the bleeding point.

Do *not* move any injured person who has a possible spinal injury. Do *not* try to push a protruding bone back under the skin. Do *not* give a fracture victim anything to eat or drink as there is a possibility that a general anaesthetic may be given at hospital. Keep the person warm and as comfortable as possible until hospital is reached; observe constantly for signs of shock.

Hypothermia/exposure The aim is to warm the body *slowly*, so move the victim to a warm place where this is possible. Remove any wet clothing and wrap the victim in a blanket or sleeping bag, preferably a space-blanket. It may also help for another person to lie next to the victim.

Do *not* let the victim walk, and do *not* try to warm the body by applying heat

directly as this could lead to a rush of blood to the extremities and therefore a reduction of blood to the brain and vital organs. Offer the victim a warm drink and not a hot one; it must not be alcoholic. If the victim is unconscious, put him in the recovery position and await medical help.

Crush injuries With a serious injury such as this the victim should *not* be moved by anybody except a trained medical team as there is a possibility of damage to the spine. Keep the victim warm with a blanket, reassure him and observe for any signs of internal bleeding or shock (pallor, sweating and a weak, rapid pulse). Provide resuscitation measures when necessary and obtain medical help immediately.

Deep cuts or wounds In the case of a deep wound with profuse bleeding, raise the injured area where possible. Apply direct, firm pressure with a sterile pad to control the bleeding and, when it appears to be under control, apply a pressure dressing. Leave the same pad *in situ* as you could disturb clots and restart bleeding if you remove it. Put other dressings on top of this one and bandage all dressings snugly. Take the victim to hospital as soon as possible. If the bleeding continues, keep applying the pressure and get medical help urgently.

Shock Shock is a failure of the circulation resulting in an inadequate supply of blood to the vital organs. It is caused when there is a lack of blood being pumped around the body due perhaps to bleeding, severe burns or electric shock. Because blood carries oxygen, failure of the circulation means that these vital organs can no longer function properly and, unless the patient is treated quickly, death may result.

Signs of shock are feeling faint or dizzy and confused (severe cases may lapse into unconsciousness), the skin becomes pale as blood is drawn away from it and the patient's pulse may grow weak as the reduced volume of blood in the arteries gives rise to low blood pressure. Breathing can become rapid and can be accompanied by sweating – a reflex response to the reduced flow of blood. It should be noted that the medical symptoms of shock bear little relationship to the normal use of the word, although the fear brought on in the patient might conceivably make the condition worse.

Treatment involves treating the cause of the trauma, reassuring the casualty as you do so. Keep the patient warm, lie him flat with his legs raised unless he is unconscious when he should be placed in the recovery position. Give nothing by mouth because of the possibility of anaesthesia at the hospital and get medical attention as soon as possible.

Remember also that it is always important in major emergencies for the rescuers to have as much information as possible of the circumstances or events surrounding the accident or incident, so that it can be passed on to the medical team when it arrives.

SUMMARY

- The rescue services tell us that many accidents at sea could easily be avoided and that most are the result of badly prepared people crewing badly prepared boats.

- The most important items of a motor boat's equipment are those selected for use in an emergency or to provide safety back-up in time of bad weather, breakdown or accident.

- Fire is always a worry at sea, so preventative measures should be taken at all times. This is where crew training is essential, but it should always be backed up with the correct equipment for dealing with the different types of fire should one start.

- Your boat should be fitted with a good-quality compass – ideally an illuminated binnacle compass positioned at the helm and backed up with a hand-held model.

- The most important channel, with priority over all others, is the Call and Distress channel – Channel 16 – and an understanding of its use and operation is essential.

7

NAVIGATING THE BOAT

The subject and science of navigation can at first seem a daunting and impenetrably complex one. Yet everyone who intends to take on the responsibility of boat ownership – especially if that boat will be cruised in tidal waters, off shore and for sea voyages – will need to learn navigation. It is beyond the scope of this book to explore and explain fully the many varied and diverse techniques which go to make up a complete navigation course. However, some of the more rudimentary items are covered, especially those relating to equipment and the types of course that can be taken by the amateur in order for him to gain the appropriate

The chart table should be as large as possible and should be kept in an uncluttered condition. The navigator should know where all his instruments are at any time, so they should be kept in order. Electronics should be within easy view and there should be some form of light for night cruising.

certificates in navigation. This chapter will explain the yachtsman's chart and the various items of equipment needed aboard the boat for safe navigation. It should give a small insight into the art and be useful as a primer for those taking a Yachtsmaster or Day Skipper course at night classes run in conjunction with the Royal Yachting Association.

The Chart

Anyone who intends to take a boat to sea needs a chart. The art of navigation is centred around the chart, and a complete understanding of it and its symbolic representations is therefore of utmost importance.

The marine chart displays a veritable wealth of information, most of which is in abbreviated form – the type of coastline, focal points and features of geography – with the make-up of the sea-bed shown in contour form so that it is almost a map of dry land in reverse! Dangers such as wrecks, shallows, sandbanks, rocks and reefs are also shown, as is tidal information, eddies, tidal streams and buoyage, together with information on radio beacons, lighthouse sectors and water depths.

Mariner's Map

With a little practice you will soon become familiar with the workings and layout of a marine chart, and will be able to assess at a glance the type of area you will be cruising into and its inherent dangers. The chart is therefore the mariner's map, showing him where he can and cannot take his boat. Whether it is used in advance of a cruise to plot a course, or for

A binnacle compass of the type that is mounted at the helm. This model from Silva is oil damped for a steady scale and is illuminated for night use. There are many compasses available today, including fluxgate electronic types.

constant referral when underway, the chart is probably the single most important item of equipment at the navigator's table – even taking into account all the sophisticated satellite and electronic navigation plotters available to him today.

To assist the navigator, the British Admiralty in the guise of the Hydrographer of the Navy is responsible for surveying the sea-bed, surrounding coastline and oceans for the charts – a sort of marine Ordnance Survey. It publishes a useful booklet entitled *Symbols and Abbreviations used on Admiralty Charts* which can be bought from most good marine chart stockists. This is very good value for money, and explains in detail the many signs and symbols used on the

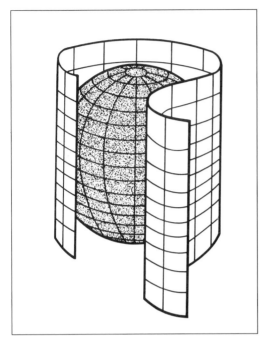

The principle of the Mercator chart. The paper chart is a representation of the global surface, as if the Earth's surface has been opened out and flattened.

chart. A reference chart and mariner's handbook is also available to help beginners understand the chart and how to get to grips with it. These books make useful reference works when learning navigation at Royal Yachting Association night classes.

There are two methods of projection or construction used in chartmaking: Mercator's projection and gnomonic projection. For our purposes, gnomonic projection charts can really be put to one side as they bear little reference to the scale of charts we use in everyday navigation.

Latitude and Longitude

If you look at a globe, you will see that the horizontal lines of latitude are all parallel with the Equator and are equidistant. However, the vertical meridians (lines of longitude) that intersect the lines of latitude at 90 degrees all eventually taper together at the north and south poles. To represent this curve of the globe on a flat surface, the chartmaker reaches a compromise whereby the meridian lines are drawn vertical, parallel and equidistant, and the distance between the lines of latitude is altered. What is displayed upon the surface of the chart is therefore correct, but you will notice that the scale at the side gradually changes from top to bottom.

Basically, therefore, with Mercator's projection the sides at the top of the chart are pulled outwards until the vertical lines are parallel, and the top and bottom edges are repositioned so that the entire area is represented as a rectangle.

Scale

Three main scales are used on marine charts. With harbour plans, a very large scale – something between 3 and 15 centimetres to 1 kilometre (2 and 10 inches to 1 mile) – is used; coastal charts cover everything from 16 to 400 kilometres (10 to 250 miles); and oceanic charts of a very small scale take in distances as great as 3,200 kilometres (2,000 miles). The scale for any particular chart is usually found up near the title and key, and is expressed as a ratio – for example, 1:1000 means that 100,000 inches on the ground (or sea) are represented by every 1 inch shown of the chart.

Two or three compass roses will appear on each chart, depending upon its size and the area covered. They basically determine the relationship of magnetic north to true north and consist of two concentric circles each divided into 360

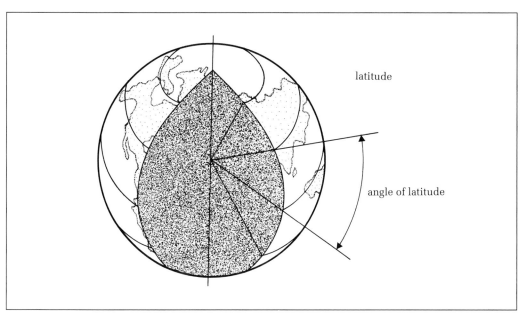

latitude

angle of latitude

Latitude. Imagine a slice taken out of the Earth; the angle between the horizontal lines of latitude and a point at the centre of the Earth is the angle of latitude.

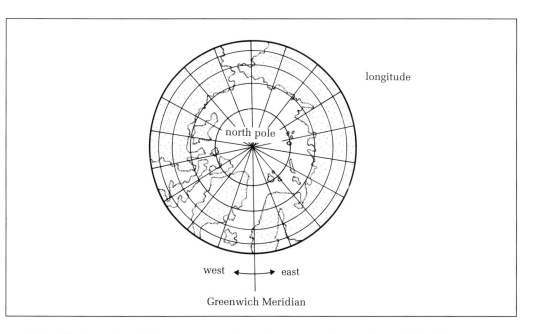

longitude

north pole

west ← → east

Greenwich Meridian

Longitude. The lines of longitude are imaginary lines drawn from pole to pole. Longitude 0° is a point at Greenwich in London known as the Greenwich Meridian.

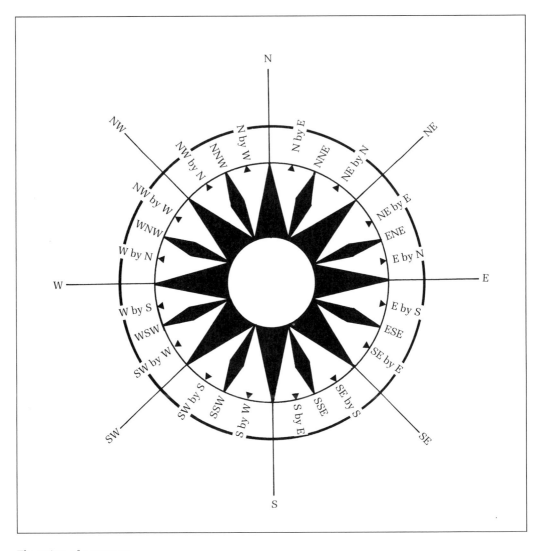

The points of a compass.

degrees. The outer circle represents true north bearings and the north-to-south line is parallel to all meridians on the chart, and at right angles to the lines of latitude. The other ring is rotated or off-set from the outer ring so that its northern point represents magnetic north. The variation in degrees can be seen from studying the two circles.

Until a few years ago all British charts showed depth in fathoms, but now most charts used throughout the world have been revised and upgraded to metric measurements showing depth and distance in metres. The mass of figures across the charted area of water depict the depths at those particular places. They are

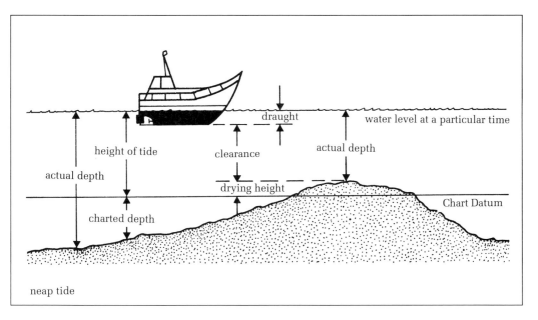

draught

water level at a particular time

height of tide

clearance

actual depth

actual depth

drying height

Chart Datum

charted depth

neap tide

Chart Datum, the mark from which tidal heights are taken and displayed on the chart as soundings.

given as being below Chart Datum (CD), which used to be taken as the level of low-water spring tides but is now the Lowest Astronomical Tide (LAT), or the lowest predicted tide that will occur during average meteorological conditions. On metric charts, soundings are shown in metres and decimetres on any depth below 20 metres – so a depth of say 8 metres 6 decimetres, or 8.6 metres, would be shown as 8_6.

Drying heights shown on the chart depict the height above low water of any given obstacle. On fathom charts the height is shown and underlined – for example, 6_2 – while on metric charts the height is shown in metres and decimetres and underlined – for example, 12_3. All drying heights are above the level of Chart Datum.

Heights of navigational features such as light beacons, lighthouses, towers and masts are given in metres and are all above the level of Mean High Water Springs (MHWS). On the coloured charts produced by Imray, the land masses are shown in green and areas drying at low water are shown in yellow. Depths that do not dry but that are under 5 metres in depth are shown in white, while all other depths are depicted in blue. On the Admiralty's coloured charts the land is buff coloured and the drying areas are green. The 10-metre contour line perimeter is in blue, and all other areas within the 5-metre contour are also blue.

Buoyage Details

The large-scale charts show all buoys and lighthouses in detail. The buoys marking harbour entrances or special channels are

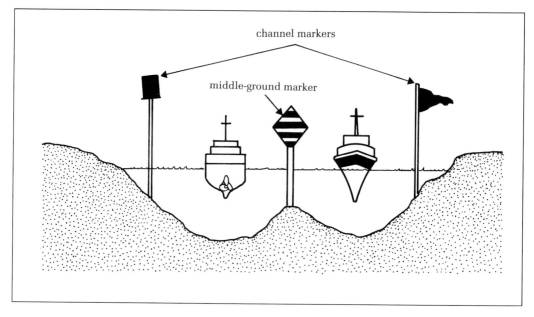

channel markers

middle-ground marker

Special marks and buoyage abound around coasts. They mark navigational hazards, sandbanks, channels and wrecks. Many hazards are marked on the chart as special symbols.

shown clearly, with appropriate daytime colouration and light information. Lighthouses are identified by their lights; no two lighthouses in one area will show similar lights. Their position on the chart is marked by a star and they are usually overprinted with a magenta or red splash.

The description of a light is shown in abbreviated terms and gives all the information required – the light's distinguishing appearance, its colour, the time taken for one complete cycle of operation, its elevation or height, the range of the light and its visibility in clear weather. For example, the Maidens lighthouse off the north-eastern tip of Ireland is indicated thus: F1 (3) 20s 29m 23M & F1 R 5s 15m 8M. This indicates that groups of three white flashes are exhibited every 20 seconds from a height of 29 metres and that they may be seen from

23 miles away in clear weather, and that a second light coloured red flashes every five seconds from a height of 15 metres and may be seen from a distance of 8 miles in fair weather. The red light usually shows over a much narrower sector than the white and warns of a dangerous approach over reefs or rocks.

Looking After Your Charts

Modern charts are expensive, and as you may eventually build up quite a collection if your cruising is extensive you will want to look after them in the best possible way.

Keep your charts as dry as possible – this may not always be practicable when navigating in inclement weather – and try to remove any wet oilskins before you lean over a chart. A plastic folder is useful

The Navstar 2000D is a popular Decca navigation receiver. It features a digital read-out and is small enough to be mounted near the helm. Repeater screens are available for other positions on board, for instance the flying bridge helm position.

A log and echo-sounder from Navico. These instruments are essential for safe and comprehensive navigation. They give details of how far the boat has travelled and the depth of water over which the boat is moving.

for protecting the chart when it is not in use, and some sort of filing system aboard will alleviate the problem of a frustrating search for a particular chart when you are in a rush. Try not to overcrease charts as they fall apart easily, and have some clear adhesive tape at hand for quick repairs. Use soft pencils when plotting and try not to score the paper too much.

The Compass

The second most important navigational instrument is the magnetic compass. The compass tells you which way your boat is heading by always pointing towards magnetic north. It can, therefore, also tell you the direction of certain objects in relation to magnetic north and your own position. By taking a sight with a hand-bearing compass (one that can be held and sighted in the hand rather than one that is attached permanently to the boat) or by using a special sighting attachment on your main compass, you can check your position at any time during the voyage in deep or shallow water.

The Calculations

Measuring distance and speed (distance divided by time) through the water is fairly easy. Modern electronic speed and distance logs have replaced the float which used to be thrown in at the bow and counted second by second down to the stern. Modern logs are very accurate and form an essential part of the navigation armament. However, if you heed the rule 'At seven knots against a four knots current, you might as well get out and walk!' and take measurements in relation

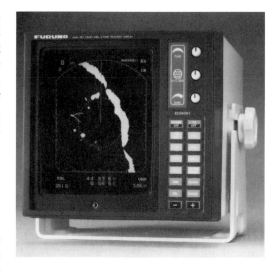

At one time a radar set on a small pleasure boat would have been unthinkable for all but the very wealthy, but the microchip has brought both size and price within the reach of most boat owners.

to the sea-bed and thus the earth's surface (which is really what the chart shows), the calculation is much more difficult.

As the above rule implies, the sea moves – and not only up and down but also backwards and forwards and even sideways. Because the sea does not provide a solid base for a ship from which it can withstand the atmosphere, it will also be subject to the wind's force and direction much more than a car or train might be on dry land. Quite apart from slowing you down or speeding you up, the wind can also move you sideways, so check the boat's wake from time to time to estimate an angle to be added to or subtracted from your calculations when giving your helmsman his compass course.

Estimated Time of Arrival (ETA)

Wind and water movement can be

measured. Wind must be observed and reasonable allowances made for it as you go. Bearing in mind that you must always work out an Estimated Time of Arrival (ETA), accuracy will increase if you listen to the broadcast shipping forecasts which will warn you of changes of speed and direction of winds along your proposed route.

Water movement, on the other hand, is more predictable since it has been observed and recorded over the years to follow a regular pattern which is not as fickle as that of the wind. This is because the major movement of water is caused by the gravitational pulls of the sun and moon – the effects we call tides. It has therefore been possible to produce tidal stream atlases which show the speed and direction of the current in any part of a popular cruising ground. These are fairly accurate since at each state of a tide, currents are found to flow in a particular direction at a certain rate. Small maps are often inset on to charts showing this information; each map relates to a successive hour before or after high tide at a given location for which times of high water are published on a daily basis. The most common location for the UK is Dover, which is known as a standard port. There are other standard ports for which times and heights of tides are quoted, and the standard port utilized for information on a particular chart or tidal atlas will be noted on that chart.

Logs

Having settled the point that measuring distance through the water is relatively easy, and having explained that you can watch the shifting of wind and look up the movement of water on tables and

A good, accurate chronometer is a useful device when navigating. This model from Plastimo also incorporates a barometer which can be used to predict weather patterns.

maps, you now need a 'log' with which to count off the miles.

On leaving harbour, but when sufficiently clear so as not to foul the line, set the pointer to zero, pay out the vane, line and sinker, and fix the line to the instrument. This is known as 'streaming' the log. When you arrive at your destination and take the log, it is known as 'handing' it. Most modern cruisers are now fitted with an electronic log to take care of the distance run. This is a device that takes signals from a small rotating paddle wheel fitted below the hull. As the boat moves through the water the wheel turns, sending signal pulses up to the computer at the helm. The computer then converts the signals into a digital or analogue readout on a gauge from which the boat's distance travelled can be read.

Instruments

Now to the chart table. Below I describe the instruments you will need to transfer your observations on to the chart and with which you shall be making the measurements that you must relay to the helmsman so that he can steer you safely on your course.

The chart table itself should be as level and firm as possible, and large enough to take a standard Admiralty or Imray chart folded once. When in use, the chart is folded back so that any two adjacent sections can be used out of four sections across, or three high. When sold to you, the chart is actually folded into eight sections across, but these are too small for convenient use. Your chart table should therefore accommodate a chart (folded), measuring some 54 centimetres (21 inches) wide by 41 centimetres (16 inches) in height. Allow for the other instruments, however, and provide a fiddle at the edge of the table to stop them rolling off on to the cabin or cockpit floor. It can be very irritating if your pencils, rubber and rules fall off the table every time the boat hits a big wave or someone steps aboard.

A good pair of parallel rules is essential. Get a pair that will not loosen up or fall apart at the crucial moment. They should not seize up so that in transferring a bearing to or from the compass rose on the chart they slip and give you a false reading. You will also need a protractor. The most convenient form is one like the 'Sestral' Luard Navigator which consists of a square protractor with an attached straight-edge which swivels about the centre-point of the protractor's compass rose. An ordinary 12-inch plastic ruler is also very useful, as is a navigator's set-

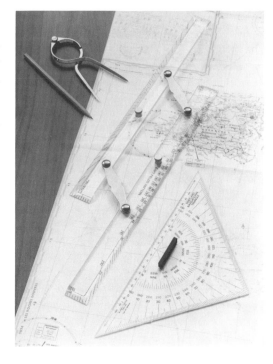

The navigator's chart instruments. A Captain Fields pattern parallel rule with a Portland triangle protractor and single-handed dividers.

square that contains protractor markings if you can't afford the better type.

Next, you will need a pair of single-hand dividers, several sharp pencils and a notebook for calculations. A pencil sharpener, a pencil rubber and a good lamp on a flexible arm also come into the chart table's inventory.

Close to the chart table is the best position for the boat's bookshelf which, ideally, should consist of a good almanac or pilot as well as logs, tide tables and any other local charts or pilot guides for the area in which you will be cruising. A *Reed's Nautical Almanac*, or the popular *Silk Cut Almanac*, may be included, and you should also carry the Admiralty tide tables as they are easier to use since they are not buried in amongst a lot of other less useful information. The best tables I have found are a small set which I purchased from my local fishing supplies shop. Naturally, you need the current tables for the year in which you are cruising. If you are making a passage across a piece of open water it is also wise to carry a copy of the *International Collision Regulations* and an international code book just in case! At the very least, learn to flash your boat's name and destination in Morse code before you set out!

For further information on navigation courses in your area (most of which are run by RYA-accredited instructors at localities all over the UK – usually during the winter months), contact your local technical college or the Royal Yachting Association itself.

A light vessel, one of the many navigation marks and buoys shown on the marine chart.

SUMMARY

- Everyone who intends to take on the responsibility of boat ownership – especially if that boat will be cruised in tidal waters, offshore and for sea voyages – will need to learn navigation.

- The art of navigation is centred around the chart, and a complete understanding of it and its symbolic representations is therefore of utmost importance.

- Until a few years ago all British charts showed depth in fathoms, but now most charts used throughout the world have been revised and upgraded to metric measures showing depth and distance in metres.

- Another important navigational instrument is the magnetic compass. It tells you which way your boat is heading by always pointing towards magnetic north. It can, therefore, also tell you the direction of certain objects in relation to magnetic north and your own position.

- A good pair of parallel rules is essential. Get a pair that will not loosen up or fall apart at the crucial moment. They should not seize up so that in transferring a bearing to or from the compass rose on the chart they slip and give you a false reading.

8

PREPARING FOR A CRUISE

Once the boat has been bought, fitted out and readied for the water, there are a number of other considerations to look at before you cast off and head for a distant destination. A well-prepared boat and crew will have a much more successful trip if some initial thought is given to the ancillary items of food, general stores, equipment and so on before setting off.

This is especially important if you are intending to go on an extended voyage, perhaps for several weeks during the summer. You will need to assess the eating requirements of your crew, when and where you will be able to replenish your food stores, and how to achieve a balanced diet for all those aboard. Think about what home comforts you will take

The wild grandeur of the Western Isles of Scotland. This view shows the entrance to the Crinan Canal in Loch Crinan south of Oban – a beautiful cruising area with some navigational interest.

aboard and how you will keep the family happy on wet days when you may be holed up in a remote marina or stuck on an anchorage through bad weather.

The best time to plan your summer trip is during the long winter months when your boat is safely in store. When the evenings start early, sit back in your favourite armchair with a glass of what you fancy, a notepad and your charts and then plot your season's boating.

Look at the Chart

To many people, half the pleasure of a cruise lies in the planning, and you can while away many pleasant cold winter evenings doing just this. There are many things to consider and once you have decided upon the general area in which you want to cruise, buy a large-scale chart of the area along with pilot books and local guides which will enable you to carry out the broad planning for the cruise. A cruise around the western isles of Scotland with its associated tidal streams, many islands and sea lochs, for example, will take quite a bit of planning if you want to get the very best out of the huge area involved.

A pilot book or guide of the region you plan to visit will allow you to look up the various ports and harbours along the way, and will help you decide which to utilize as an overnight stop or as a base for a couple of days' exploration of the surrounding countryside. Armed with the chart and the pilot book, you can settle down to your first evening of planning, but before you start here is a word of caution: do not be over ambitious. It is very easy to get carried away when you look at the chart and measure off dis-

tances which, when combined with the appealing photographs and attractive descriptions in the pilot book, might make you want to squeeze more and more into your fortnight's cruise. You will end up with a cruise plan that occupies every hour of every day and which leaves you no margin for error, bad weather conditions or, perhaps more importantly, for real relaxation. With this sort of programme you will end up coming back to work for a rest – certainly not the reason for going on any holiday. However, there is no reason why you should not make one or two fairly ambitious passages during the cruise, and for many this can be part of the attraction.

Time Limits and Weather

The main things to remember when planning are the two factors which will dictate what you can achieve on a cruise, namely the weather and the fact that you may have a deadline by which you have to get back to your home port. You cannot do a great deal about the weather, but at least you can make allowances for possible bad weather in your planning. This way, any bad weather will not come as too much of a shock. It certainly shouldn't put you under any pressure to start taking chances in order to get back home in the time allowed.

Because the deadline to get home is always hanging over you, you may feel obliged to allow two or three days at the end of the cruise to complete the final few kilometres. This means that you may end up getting back a couple of days early and finishing off your cruise in a rather flat way by just cruising the same old boring home waters. The alternative is to plan your cruise so that you make your way

Try to plan your cruising itinerary so that you arrive at a safe harbour each evening – unless, of course, your penchant is for quiet anchorages. This view shows Porthmadog Harbour on the north-west coast of Wales.

back home in gradual stages, ending up on the final day or two with only a comparatively short passage to make, and preferably one which is not likely to be too prone to bad weather conditions.

Longer Passages

It is probably best to make any long passages at the beginning of the cruise. This has two advantages: it gets you out of your normal cruising ground in the quickest possible time, and you will be able to reach the furthest point of your destination in the early days of the holiday. In this way you can work your way back to-

wards the home port in a series of gentle daily stages, perhaps covering 50 or 65 kilometres (30 or 40 miles) each day, and leaving plenty of time in harbour to enjoy the local sights and scenery. If, on this enjoyable part of the cruise, you then find yourself stuck with a day or even a couple of days of bad weather, it is not too difficult to make up time simply by covering two of the legs in one day.

Your day's mileage will depend on your boat and on your personal preference, but on average around 80 or 105 kilometres (50 to 65 miles) each day will be a comfortable distance for even a slower displacement-type boat. This sort of mileage will let you keep to your proposed schedule without too much difficulty. Even on the final legs you will still have this option open, and as bad weather rarely lasts for more than twenty-four hours during the summer months, you needn't get too nervous about missing your deadline for getting home.

Greater Detail

Once the general plan of each day has been settled, you can go out and buy more detailed charts and start to work out some of the interesting navigation problems you might have to face. Try to get the most detailed charts possible for the cruising area in which you will work as these can add considerably to your enjoyment and will let you navigate at close quarters, perhaps exploring interesting areas that are not covered in enough detail by larger-scale charts.

Having worked out the general pattern of your cruise, start looking for options which might be open to you if the weather turns foul. There is not much point in cruising doggedly up an exposed coast-line in bad weather when there might be a much more pleasant option open to you simply by keeping under the lee of the land. These options can usually be decided on the spur of the moment after you have seen what the conditions are like, but you cannot use them unless you have the right charts on board.

For beginners to motorboating, the quieter rivers and canals might be an attraction. The River Severn near Tewkesbury is shown here. It connects with the sea at the Bristol Channel and is navigable as far as Stourport where, if your boat has a narrow beam, you can lock up into the canal system.

Stocking Up

With the planning and navigation details over, it is now time to look at the logistics of the cruise. You will obviously need to top up your boat with fresh water and fuel at some time during the fortnight. Fresh water is rarely a problem, but fuel can sometimes be difficult to obtain, particularly if you are cruising in a remote area. Studying the pilot book, make out a list of the harbours where fuel is easily obtainable. In many of the smaller harbours you can only get fuel by carrying it in cans down from the local garage – pretty tough when you need 100 gallons or more! If you are cruising to remote areas where there are small harbours with few facilities, you may have to plan at least one call into a major port in order to get fuel from a pump alongside.

In your study of ports and harbours along the way, facilities such as hotels and restaurants might loom quite large in your priorities. Personally, I like to eat out as much as possible when on my holidays to make a break from routine, and many will find that they miss some of the luxuries in life having lived within the confines of a boat for a week or so. If this is the case then a night spent in a hotel with the luxury of a bath will give you a bit of breathing space. If food looms large in your priorities when you are cruising, then a restaurant and hotel guide will be a useful addition to your onboard library. Some hotels and restaurants popular with cruising people even keep a listening watch on the local VHF channel so that you can book your table *en route*, as it were. You can also make a land link telephone call from your VHF if required.

Food and Drink

You will need to stock up with fresh food on many occasions during your cruise, unless you enjoy eating out of tins and dehydrated packets (there are actually some excellent new dry foods available), and one reason for not being too ambitious in your plans is to allow time each day when you are in harbour to go ashore to shop. It is amazing how much time this takes, and you do need to build it into your schedule if you do not want to run out of food.

Different people have different ideas about their daily time schedule when on holiday. I personally don't like to be too regimented – after all it is supposed to be a rest from routine! Some like to leave harbour comparatively early in the morning so that they arrive at their next port by early afternoon, and I think this approach has a lot to recommend it. It certainly gives you plenty of time to settle any problems which might arise in the new port, such as difficulty in finding a berth, or looking for fuel or water before the services close. Your alternative is to leave all this until the next morning, but you may find it frustrating getting away late. If it is dark when you get to your next evening port of call you will also miss out on the relaxing evening meal and drinks that you were looking forward to. Much will depend on your individual priorities and the way you like to organize things, but certainly you must allow ample time during normal working hours to fit in shopping and other requirements.

Money

You are bound to need money on your cruise and this is something to think about in advance, particularly if you are going abroad. In home waters credit cards and cheques will probably cope with most of your needs, even if you face the misfortune of having to pay for extra fuel. If you are going abroad, however, you need to look at the money situation a bit more carefully, and whilst credit cards can work wonders these days, you might like to back them up with traveller's cheques for emergencies. When using credit cards abroad, always ask about exchange rates and currency transfers as you might end up paying a premium – a big shock when your next statement comes in. Of course, you will also need some cash in the currency of the country you will visit, but the traveller's cheques

can provide a useful emergency fund. If you carry these, however, do check up on the bank opening hours in the particular country you are visiting as they can vary considerably.

Sitting down to pore over charts in the long winter evenings can give a great deal of pleasure, but you also face the more onerous task of getting the boat itself ready for the job. During a two-week cruise you may well cover more miles than you do in the rest of the season, so it pays to have the boat technically correct and serviced before you depart. Much of this work will be done during the winter overhaul and is covered fully in the next chapter.

SUMMARY

- A well-prepared boat and crew will have a much more successful trip if some initial thought is given to the ancillary items of food, general stores, equipment and so on before setting off.

- The best time to plan your summer trip is during the long winter months when your boat is safely in store.

- A pilot book or guide of the region you plan to visit will allow you to look up the various ports and harbours along the way and will help you decide which to utilize as an overnight stop or as a base for a couple of days' exploration of the surrounding countryside.

- Your day's mileage will depend on your boat and on your personal preference, but on average 80 to 105 kilometres (50 to 65 miles) each day will be a comfortable distance for even a slower displacement-type boat.

- If food looms large in your priorities when you are cruising, then a restaurant and hotel guide will be a useful addition to your onboard library.

9
CARE AND MAINTENANCE

The care and maintenance of a motor boat is an essential part of boat ownership. There are few people today who can simply call in at their local boat-yard and ask the service manager to give the boat a pre-season service or store it for them at the end of a hard summer's cruising. Apart from being expensive, this takes away what is probably one of the most pleasurable aspects of boat ownership – the ability to get your hands dirty by servicing the engine, fitting new items of equipment and generally taking care of your pride and joy. If you remember from the early chapters in this book just how much time and money can be put into boating, it only follows that proper care and attention should be given to the

The care and maintenance of any boat is essential to its longevity. Just look at what has happened to this cruiser whose canopy has been ripped off during a gale. The owners have obviously not visited it for some time and the varnish work has suffered. How much water has entered the bilges and how has the engine been affected?

various parts of your investment. Another reason, and one which is more important still, is that the aspects of safety should be considered. A boat that goes to sea with an engine badly in need of a service, flares that are past their use-by date and electrics that could cause a fire at the first opportunity is undoubtedly a potential death-trap for its owner and his crew.

There is insufficient room in this chapter to go into great detail on every single aspect of the care and repair of a motor boat, but we can look at most areas which can be covered by the DIY boat owner who has a certain amount of skill and a good set of tools. The two main points in a boat's maintenance calendar come at the beginning and at the end of the boating season. When the season finishes the boat needs to be put through a fairly rigorous procedure (commonly known as wintering) which will protect its systems and fabric from the ravages of the weather throughout this time. In the spring, this wintering procedure is reversed and the boat, its engine and various internal systems, such as water, electrics and plumbing, are restored to full use. Because these activities encompass many of the procedures and checks needed in looking after a boat generally, the following maintenance account is written as if a boat was being prepared for a new season.

Whether the boat is moored inland on a river, lake or at a canal-side marina, the battering it can receive from even the mildest of winters is amazing. Canopies can be ripped and torn away by the wind, thereby exposing the cockpit of the boat; and its associated timber, ropes and mooring lines can become frayed; bilges may be flooded because the bilge pump was not left working or the supply battery went flat; water systems may have frozen and subsequently burst at the thaw. The list is endless and *very* expensive to correct. Many of these troubles can, however, be prevented, or at least alleviated, by a proper programme of maintenance, so let us now examine the various procedures for getting the boat in order for a new cruising year.

Damp

Damp is one of the worst offenders after a long winter, so when you first arrive at the boat open all the curtains and windows to let in some fresh air. Prudent owners will have left a small ventilation space open at the end of the previous season, so a musty smell should not be present. They will also have removed all the bedding and upholstery, or at least turned the seat sections on their sides to let some air circulate. Take these outside and let them air for a while, wiping away any dampness that may have formed through condensation on PVC seat covers. The curtains can be taken home and washed.

Windows

While you are dealing with the cabin windows, examine the seals on rubber-frame types – has there been any leaking? Sealant can be used to fill small cracks, but note any rubber that has perished – the seal may need to be replaced. On aluminium-frame windows (which are used on the majority of boats today) clean out the sliders and tracks, removing debris from drainage channels and holes. Finish the windows by giving the glass a good polish.

Decks

Sweep the decks of leaves, twigs and slime. If running water is available, hose down the decks and superstructure, scrubbing them with a small brush or bristled broom. Painted non-slip surfaces can be given a fresh coat of non-slip paint and stick-on non-slip strips should be replaced if peeling. If there are any additional areas that could do with a bit of non-slip paint then deal with these also, or apply some special self-adhesive strips which are available for awkward areas.

Deck Fittings

Deck fittings should be checked for wear or play, especially sea railings and their support stanchions that take a lot of punishment from people climbing aboard. Giving the cleats, bollards and safety rails a good shake should be enough to tell you if they require tightening from below. If, when doing this, you discover that a fastening has been leaking (tell-tale rust or discoloration), remove the fitting, clean the area above and below, then apply a fresh layer of waterproof sealant to rebed the fitting before retightening it on to its backing plate. Put on enough sealant so that any excess is squeezed out as you tighten, a sure sign that you have achieved a watertight joint.

Check stanchions and wire railing at the points where they fix to the deck or cabin topsides. Swaged terminals should be inspected for cracking and remade as required. If the life-buoy was not removed at the end of the previous season, inspect its life-line and the security of the clasp bracket.

The anchor winch should be stripped down and its individual bearings and brushes cleaned in petrol. Grease these upon reassembly using the lubricant recommended by the manufacturer. Clean out the chain locker and inspect the anchor's shackle and chain.

The Hull

If the boat has been kept afloat during the winter, slip it now and remove any algae or barnacles from the underside. Give the entire hull a fresh coat of an appropriate anti-fouling and, if it is a GRP boat, check at the same time for any signs of osmosis, deep scratching or chipped laminate and repair them before applying the paint.

A closer examination of the rudder and propellers can now be undertaken, checking for wear in the through-hull bearing and rudder cups.

Through-hull fittings such as the log impeller, echo-sounder transducer and sea-cock outlets should not, of course, be painted. Transducers can be cleaned carefully and polished for maximum performance. Brass, bronze and alloy fittings should be inspected for signs of cathodic action and the protective anodes checked for wear – replace them if they are about three-quarters wasted. Don't forget the ones on the propshaft and rudder!

Pump out any accumulated water from the bilges and give them a clean using a proprietary detergent. Remove debris from limber holes and make a cursory check of the bulkhead fixing point and compartments for any signs of movement or fracture. Whilst in the bilge, examine the pump and its float switch assembly, and check that the outlet pipe is not kinked, that it is free from debris and that the clip attaching it to the hull-skin fitting is tight.

The bilges under the engine are always susceptible to oil and dirt. Prevent this by fitting a special piece of reusable bilge sponge which soaks up the oil.

If any keel bolts are visible, inspect for rust – if they are suspect then have a proper X-ray search done, especially if the boat is very old. An X-ray search should be carried out every four years or so as a matter of course.

Engines

Inboards

The inboard should be sluiced down and degreased with a proprietary degreasing agent, before being washed off and dried. It must be de-inhibited – a reversal of the procedure carried out at the end of the last season when the boat was stored in its 'winter state'.

Drain out any rust-proofing oil that may

have been inserted into the engine during the last season by removing the sump plug or by using an automatic oil-sump suction pump (much simpler and less messy), then flush out the block by using a flushing agent which can be bought from most garages. Replace the plugs and refill the sump with fresh oil of the correct grade and type. The gearbox should also be drained of inhibiting fluid and refilled to the correct level with its own special lubricant.

Check the fuel filter, emptying any sediment from the collection bowl underneath. Remember that before starting the engine the fuel system should be bled to remove trapped air from pipes and injectors. The instructions for this simple job will be found in your engine handbook along with other useful service tips. It may also be wise to take off the injectors and have them sent away to be serviced professionally by a dealer.

Reconnect the cooling water system

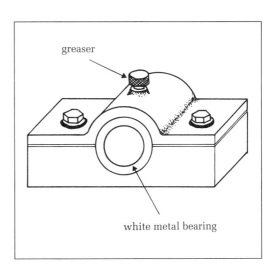

greaser

white metal bearing

Daily maintenance checks on the engine should include giving the stern-gland greaser a turn to inject lubrication into the bearing below.

and examine the water pump and its impeller for damage and wear. Once filled and the engine started, check the level of the cooling water and top up as necessary. There is no need to drain off the anti- freeze in your cooling system as most types can now be left in all year round. Check the rubber hoses and their securing clips for signs of perishing, splits or rusting respectively. On petrol engines,

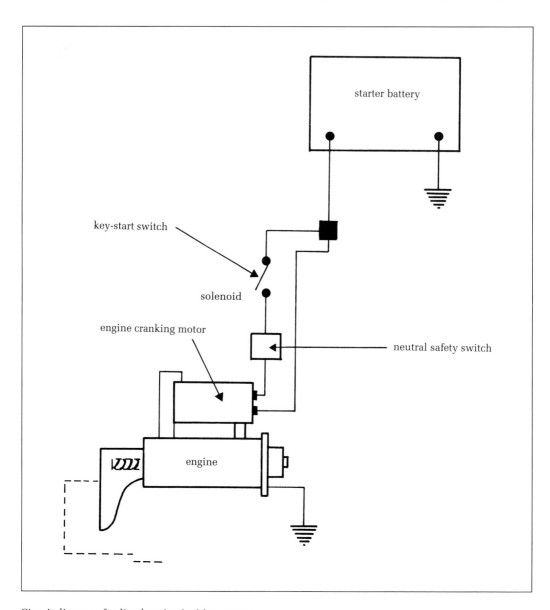

Circuit diagram of a diesel engine ignition system.

At the start and end of each cruising season, clean and service the engine, replacing filters and oil. Do the same for the outboard motor.

take out the plugs and turn over the engine to remove any oil which may have been inserted into the cylinders at the start of the winter. Replace the plugs, setting the electrode gaps to the correct size using feeler gauges, and do not overtighten them – if in doubt use a torque wrench set to the plug setting given in your handbook.

Replace the fuel-fitter element as well as oil and air filters, and then check the level of oil in the oil-bath air cleaner if fitted (usually only on older engines). Touch up any chipped paintwork, wipe over the engine with an oiled cloth and give the ignition and starter motor leads a spray with a waterproofing agent. Remove any cardboard covers placed to keep out frost from air-intake ports.

Outdrive Units

If your boat is fitted with an outdrive, reduce the level of oil in the gearcase to its correct *summer* level, check the rubber bellows for perishing and wear, and touch up any chipped paint with an appropriate enamel. Remember to examine the sacrificial anode on the leg for signs of corrosion. If it is badly wasted, it should be replaced. Never paint over the anode or it will not do its job!

Once the engine has warmed up, monitor the oil pressure, temperature and the state of the batteries by observing the ammeter. Also check on the discharge of water from the tell-tale pipe on externally cooled engine installations.

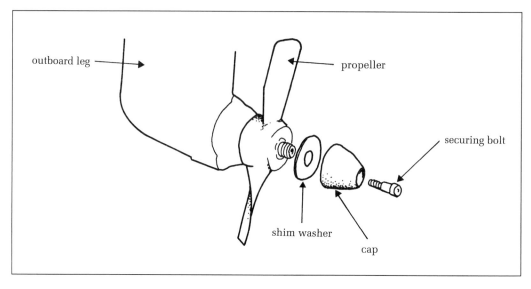

Component parts of an outboard lower leg. These should be removed periodically to check for fishing line or wire that may have become trapped behind the prop. Greasing the shaft also helps to keep things running smoothly.

Outboards

If the boat is fitted with an outboard motor, this will probably have been taken home for storage over the winter. Now is the time to bring it back to the boat and prepare it for the new year.

Firstly, take out the spark plugs and turn over the engine a few times to remove any oil from the cylinders. Fit correctly gapped new plugs and check the condition of ignition leads and plug caps. Change the gearbox lubricant by removing the appropriate screws and refill using your usual outboard lower leg lubricant. At the same time watch for signs of a worn gasket seal, shown up by the presence of water in the oil which usually turns a milky white.

Grease the carburettor linkages, throttle and gearshift controls and cables, transom clamp screws and the main swivel bracket using waterproof marine-grade grease. If your outboard is a four-stroke, change the sump oil and reset the valve clearances using the figures given in the handbook. With a two-stroke engine, make sure that any fuel left in the integral tank at the top of the engine is shaken thoroughly and remixed before you start the engine as the oil tends to separate and sink to the bottom of the solution if left for a long period. Petrol should also be shaken before use so that the tiny, hard crystals that sometimes form in the bottom of undisturbed cans are dispersed.

Wipe the motor and run it up to temperature *in situ* on the boat, checking that the cooling system is working properly. If fitted, the sacrificial anode should be inspected and replaced if it is badly corroded.

Electrical System

The heart of any boat is its electrical system. This is also one of its most vulnerable parts – constant dampness, water sloshing around the bilges, condensation and a general salt-laden atmosphere all add up to potential problems for the on-board electrics. Corrosion caused by dissimilar metals combining with the salt water to form mini-batteries may also cause havoc with fixtures, fittings and electrical equipment. It is therefore essential to have a working knowledge of the electrical system in order to maintain it correctly as well as trouble-shoot if things go wrong.

Maintenance

Electrical systems and water do not mix, so boat electrics need extra special care if they are to perform their duties in a safe and reliable manner. Good installation practice and simple maintenance can make the difference between trouble-free cruising and endless problems.

Starting with the first link in the chain, the batteries should be mounted securely, preferably out of the engine compartment. A glass-fibre box is an ideal housing for batteries as the resin is unaffected by acid. A plywood box glassed inside with two layers of chopped strand mat and resin is simple to make and provides a secure home for the batteries when bolted down in a suitably ventilated compartment. A lid is an important item which should be included in home-built battery boxes; it prevents metal items such as spanners falling on top of the battery and causing a massive short circuit – if this happened it could start a fire or cause the battery to explode and spray acid in all directions.

Charging

An important point to note when planning an installation is that batteries will give off relatively large quantities of hydrogen gas during high-rate charging – for example, after a night of watching the television with all the accommodation lights blazing. If it is essential to mount the batteries in the engine compartment they should be kept well away from hot areas, and a sparkproof fan should be arranged to extract any fumes from the compartment.

After charging the batteries using a mains charger, it is always important to switch off the mains power to the charger before removing the crocodile clips from the battery terminals; failure to remember this can lead to an explosion, as the small arc which is created as the clips are removed is sufficient to ignite the gas produced when charging. The explosion will destroy the battery and cover anyone in the vicinity with hot acid. The consequences of this can be quite catastrophic – severe burns and possibly the loss of eyesight.

Isolation Switches

Cut-out switches to isolate the batteries completely from the electrical system should be heavy enough to carry all the current demands from the craft, including the starter current. Models are available to fit directly on to the battery terminal posts or for remote mounting. The latter type can be obtained in models for switching in two batteries, either separately or in parallel pairs. The drawback with this type is that longer battery leads are required, travelling from battery to master switch and then to the starter motor via

121

the solenoid. Over very long runs this can lead to a voltage drop and resultant starting problems, so care is required when sighting cut-out switches to keep cable runs to a minimum.

Battery Maintenance

All the terminals on batteries and isolating switches should be clean and kept greased with either petroleum jelly or one of the proprietary battery terminal greases available from motor-accessory shops. Battery electrolyte levels should be checked as part of the weekly engine service schedule of oil and water levels, and topped up as necessary using de-ionised water. Any sudden drop in electrolyte level will indicate a damaged battery casing or even severe over-charging, causing the plates in the battery to buckle.

Modern low-maintenance batteries should not require topping up more than about once a year, but if an overcharge situation arises then even these will need more frequent attention – a clear in-dication that the entire system needs checking. Maintenance-free batteries (which are, of course, more expensive) can almost be fitted and forgotten, but even the terminals of these will need to be cleaned and greased occasionally.

Joints and Connections

Good connections are essential for re-liable electrical systems – not only for the heavy items just mentioned, but also for all equipment down to the smallest light fitting. It is tempting to twist a couple of wires together and bind them with insulating tape, and although the item will no doubt work quite satisfactorily, by

Check the level of electrolyte in the engine batteries, and top up as necessary using fresh distilled water. It might also be a good idea to check the specific gravity of the battery acid using a hydrometer purchased from a motor accessory shop.

using this method you will have built in a potential failure point and fire hazard. Insulating tape does not last long in a hot and oily atmosphere, and, once it has dropped off, the bare wires can easily short out and cause a fire, or just corrode away to break the circuit. With the wide variety of crimp terminal kits readily available today there is no excuse for making bad connections. Once upon a time all connections had to be soldered, but a proper crimped connector is as reliable as a good soldered one, and in any case it is much better than a bad connection.

Crimp terminal kits usually include a

cutting/crimping tool and a selection of terminals, including bullet connectors (male and female for in-line connections), spade connectors (also male and female, generally for equipment connections but also for in-line), and eyelets in various sizes (mainly for equipment connections which do not accept spades).

Finally, on the subject of connections, there are the plastic connecting strips which have many uses as cable junctions and even in-line connectors. They are easy to use and infinitely preferable to the 'twist and insulate' joint mentioned earlier. They are also good items to have as part of your electrical spares kit.

Dynamos and Alternators

Older dynamo models had an oiling point on their back bearing which required a few drops of oil during service, but later types and alternators are now generally maintenance-free apart from the need for an occasional clean and spray with a waterproofing agent. Belts, of course, should be checked during engine service. Dynamo belts require 2.5 centimetres (1 inch) of up-and-down movement on the longest straight section, while alternator belts need to be tighter with 1 centimetre (½ inch) of movement. Starter motors (generally installed at the lower end of the engine near the bilge) should be checked to ensure that they are not swimming in oily bilge water. Once again, a good squirt of waterproofing agent both inside and out should keep it operating smoothly. After using one of these sprays on any equipment, allow about half an hour before operating as the solvents in the spray are highly inflammable and will be ignited by sparks in the motor. A spray over all exposed contacts and connections

in the electrical system will help to keep corrosion at bay, especially if done during laying up and refitting.

Finally, remember that the electrical system is a working part of the boat and should be given the same care and attention as any other on-board system. It will then respond with reliable service.

AC Generators

More and more boats are now being fitted with a second, AC circuit of 240 volts which allows the owner to use a variety of appliances which previously could only be used in the home. Many marinas and boat-yards now have 240-volt AC supplies wired directly to special outlet sockets installed on their pontoon berths; all the boat owner has to do is plug in a fly-lead from the boat to this outlet to get on-board 'mains'. This situation is ideal when carrying out any form of maintenance and repairs to the boat, as electric drills, sanders and jig saws can be used to cut down on time and effort. You will also be able to boil a kettle and even microwave your dinner!

The on-board AC circuit usually takes the form of a ring main similar to those installed in the majority of houses. An armoured inlet socket is fitted to the boat, usually on deck in a weatherproofed position where it can be accessed easily. The input cables – live, neutral and earth – are normally contained in one cable which is fed to a small domestic fuse box, this having one circuit fused at 30 amps for the power sockets and another at 5 amps for lighting. It should be remembered that the 240-volt AC circuit has *no* connection whatsoever with the battery-supplied 12-volt DC circuit, and never should.

Another useful way of supplying 240-volt AC aboard the boat is to install a generator. These come in all shapes and sizes from large fixed installations supplying around 7 kilowatts to small, portable models with outputs of 400 watts. The latter are particularly attractive on smaller boats, and are sufficient to run small power tools and to keep the batteries topped up as they also have a 12-volt DC outlet. The smaller generators are fairly cheap, thus making a 'mains' supply on board an attractive proposition.

The 240-volt mains circuit can be a potential safety hazard if not installed absolutely correctly. Earth leakage circuit breakers are now a common safety item, especially on equipment in the home, such as lawn mowers, and these are an excellent safeguard against shocks on board boats. Maintenance on these systems is restricted to ensuring that all connections are in good condition, especially the earth bonding lead, and that the wiring is not chafing through at any point or dangerously close to any hot areas of the engine compartment.

Domestic Water System

The water system on board will need to be checked before the tanks are filled with fresh drinking water. The system will have been wintered by draining down the tanks, pipes and pump, so reconnect the hoses to the main pump and fit new securing clips if required. Refit the inlet pipe to the water heater and tighten any bleed screws that you left open when draining the heater's integral jacket. Fill the water system in the usual way and run the taps for about fifteen minutes to help remove any bacteria or dirt from the

Drain off the main domestic water supply by removing the outlet pipe from the water pump.

system. Make sure that your reconnected pipes do not leak, see that the taps turn off correctly and, in the case of plastic couplings on pipework, that each one is screwed up tight.

Toilets

Swill out the portable chemical toilet and recharge it with fresh water and the correct solution of sanitary fluid. Mop the toilet/shower compartment floor and walls, then clean out the shower tray and hand basin. Wash everything with disinfectant and place a new air freshener in the compartment. If your toilet is of the pump-out variety or a flushing type, have it serviced if you forgot to do so at the end of the previous year.

Galleys

Wipe down work surfaces, cooker and

sink, and pour a strong bleach solution down the waste pipe. The refrigerator should be opened up and washed out thoroughly with a mild solution of bicarbonate of soda and water.

Finally, check the gas installation, couplings to the cooker, heaters and gas bottles. Suspect leaks can usually be detected by brushing a solution of soapy water over the suspected area with a paint brush. A proprietary product in an aerosol can is also available for this job and is a good item to keep on board.

Safety Equipment

Return all the dry-powder fire extinguishers to the boat; they should have been checked and serviced by the dealer over the winter. Fit the fire blanket back in the galley and the flare pack in its proper place near the helm after checking for omissions and use-by dates. The first-aid box should also be checked and any missing contents replaced. Refit the life-raft after having it professionally serviced

and check emergency rations and the fabric of all life-jackets on the boat. Any safety harnesses or life-lines should be examined and the stitching on the webbing repaired if badly worn. Also check the clips and fasteners for ease of operation and for any signs of corrosion.

Finally, there are one or two smaller items which tend to be overlooked but which are vital to the safety of boat and crew. Charts should be checked for excessive wear and replaced if badly folded or torn. The latest editions of the nautical almanacs, which contain much useful information for the navigator, should be bought, along with up-to-date tide tables. Any notices to mariners which may have appeared through the winter months should be used to mark up and correct each chart to which they refer. Navigation instruments should be taken back on board, pencils replaced if stubby and any broken or damaged devices such as dividers, protractor or parallel rules repaired or replaced. Check the boat's tool box, replacing any items that were taken away for use at home.

SUMMARY

- The care and maintenance of a motor boat is an essential part of boat ownership.

- If any keel bolts are visible, inspect for rust – if they are suspect then have a proper X-ray search done, especially if the boat is very old. An X-ray search should be carried out every four years or so as a matter of course.

- If the boat is fitted with an outboard motor, this will probably have been taken home for storage over the winter. Now is the time to bring it back to the boat and prepare it for the new year.

- The heart of any boat is its electrical system. This is also one of its most vulnerable parts – constant dampness, water sloshing around the bilges, condensation and a general salt-laden atmosphere all add up to potential problems for the on-board electrics.

GLOSSARY

Abaft Behind.

Abeam At one side of the centre section of the boat.

Adrift A boat or item that is loose or unmoored.

Aft The back of the boat.

Ahead In the front part of the boat.

Amidships In the centre of the boat.

Astern Behind the boat; reverse.

Athwartships Across the boat.

Awash At the same level as the water.

Ballast Weight placed in the lower part of a boat to give stability and trim.

Bar A shallow spit of sand or mud across a harbour entrance.

Beam Width of the boat, usually measured from a central position.

Bear off Move off from a quayside mooring.

Bight A loop in the centre section of a rope.

Bilge The bottom of the boat's interior.

Bitter end The last link in the anchor chain.

Boat hook A pole or staff with a hook at one end.

Bollard Stout mooring post.

Bow The front of a boat.

Broach The boat swings quickly side-on to the oncoming waves.

Bulkhead An internal partition separating cabins and so on.

Bulwarks A low, solid railing around the deck area.

Buoy A floating navigation mark.

Casting off Letting go a mooring rope.

Cleat A special deck fitting to which ropes can be tied off and secured.

Coaming The raised section surrounding the cockpit.

Cockpit The area (usually at the stern) in which the crew sits to control the boat.

Dinghy A small, open craft used on larger boats as a tender.

Displacement The boat's total weight.

Draft The amount of the boat that sits below the water-line.

Fairlead A special fitting at deck level into which the mooring ropes are guided.

Fairway The unencumbered, navigable channel.

Fathom A unit of measurement equivalent to 1.8 metres (6 feet).

Fender Plastic air-filled bags used to protect the sides of a vessel.

Fiddle rail Bolt-on attachment to the cooker to stop pans from sliding off it.

Freeboard The amount of measurable deck above the water-line.

Galley The cooking area aboard a boat.

Gimbals A swinging pivot which keeps the compass *et al* upright at all times.

Ground tackle The anchor and its associated warps and chain.

Gunwale The joint between the topsides and the deck.

Heads The boat's toilet facility.

Helm The steering position.

Holding ground The type of sea-bed used when anchoring.

Jury rig A rudder, mast or similar, made from other parts of the boat in an emergency.

Keel The spine of the boat or the weighted section under the hull.

Knot A unit of speed equivalent to 1 nautical mile per hour.

Lee side The side of the boat opposite the wind.

Leeward Away from the direction of the wind.

Leeway The sideways drift of the boat caused by the action of the wind.

Life-jacket A safety device that keeps a person afloat.

Log An electrical or mechanical device used to measure the boat's speed and distance through the water.

Logbook A record kept aboard of navigational details of a voyage.

Make fast To secure a warp to a cleat or bollard.

Mooring Tying up alongside or to a swinging buoy.

Nautical mile A unit of measurement equal to approximately 1,830 metres (2,000 yards).

Outboard Outside the boat; portable petrol-driven propulsion unit.

Overfalls A confused area of water where two tidal systems meet.

Port The left-hand side of a boat when facing forward.

Pulpit The guard-rail that surrounds the bow area.

Pushpit The guard-rail that surrounds the stern area.

Quarter The rear corner of a boat.

Riding light The white anchor light.

Rowlock A swivel bracket on the gunwale of a rowing boat in which the oar is held.

Rubbing strake Timber, plastic or rubber fendering in a strip to protect the sides of a boat.

Rudder A flat blade which swivels underwater at the stern and which is used for steering the boat.

Scuppers Drain holes low down in the bulwarks.

Set of tide The direction in which the tide runs.

Shackle A metal fitting with a screw gate.

Shank The long arm of an anchor.

Sheer To swing about the anchor.

Shoal water Very shallow, fast water.

Slack water The period at which there is no measurable tidal flow.

Sounding The depth of water shown on the chart.

Spring An extra one or two mooring lines that prevent fore and aft movement on a quayside.

Stanchion A stout post supporting the sea railing.

Starboard The right-hand side of the boat when facing forward.

Steerage way Sufficient speed to allow the rudder to alter the boat's course.

Stem The front of the bow.

Stern The back part of the boat.

Tender A small boat carried aboard and used for getting ashore.

Tiller The long shaft of wood or metal connected to the rudder and used for steering.

Topsides The section of the boat above the water-line.

Transducer A device used to relay and emit echo signals for soundings.

Underway The boat, when moving through the water unattached.

Up and down When the anchor warp is in a vertical attitude.

Wind rode The boat when lying to wind at anchor.

Yaw To wander either side of a predetermined course.

INDEX